THE ROAD TO NO. 1

THE TENNESSEE VOLS' GLORIOUS JOURNEY TO THE 1998 NATIONAL CHAMPIONSHIP

AN EPIC SPORTS BOOK

FROM THE SPORTS PAGES OF

The Knoxville News-Sentinel
The Commercial Appeal

SCRIPPS HOWARD

Corporate Sponsors

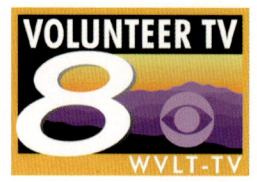

Photo Gallery

● **GATOR BAIT:** 107,000-plus Vol fans were on hand to watch the end of Florida's win streak over UT.

● **VOLMANIA:** By November, the Vols' magical journey to No. 1 had unleashed an excitement that had never been seen before among the Orange Nation.

The Road to No. 1

● **END OF THE ROAD:** John Ward (top) and his partner Bill Anderson concluded their 31-year career of broadcasting Vols football at the Fiesta Bowl.

The Road to No. 1

● **FIELD GENERAL:** Tee Martin stepped out of Peyton Manning's shadows and led the Vols to a national title.

● **WORK HORSE:** When heralded halfback Jamal Lewis was injured, Travis Henry stepped in and carried the Vols to greatness.

● **LIGHTNING:** Peerless Price's acrobatic catches and blazing speed made him the "Go-to" guy when a big play had to be made.

● **FEARLESS:** Phillip Fulmer's devoted work ethic pushed the Vols to be champions.

The Knoxville News-Sentinel
204 WEST CHURCH AVENUE
KNOXVILLE, TN 37950

JANUARY 5, 1999

THE 47-YEAR WAIT WAS WORTH IT.

The University of Tennessee Volunteers, for the first time since 1951, are the National Champions of collegiate football.

And there was nothing unlucky about the number 13 as Tennessee defeated Florida State in the Fiesta Bowl to cap a perfect 13-0 season that culminated in the elusive, but prized, national title.

The Knoxville News-Sentinel with an assist from its sister newspaper, The Commercial Appeal in Memphis, is pleased to present *"The Road to No. 1,"* the story of the Volunteers' triumphant journey to football's ultimate bragging rights of saying, "We're No. 1."

"The Road to No. 1" is a sequel to our earlier publication, *"The Road to Glory,"* that chronicled the Tennessee's successful 12-0 1998 football season and SEC championship. We now add the final chapter to this wonderful season with a look at the entire road to the National Championship.

A team of nine News-Sentinel writers and photographers was on hand at the Fiesta Bowl when Coach Phillip Fulmer's Vols wrapped up a wonderful season. They were Sports Editor John Adams, sports writers Mike Strange, Gary Lundy, Mike Griffith, and Dan Fleser plus columnist Sam Venable, and photographers Byron Small, Michael Patrick and Joe Howell. The Commercial Appeal's sports writers David Williams, Geoff Calkins, and Don Wade also contributed to this effort.

In addition to those at the game, it is appropriate to recognize the Sports Department staffers who also contributed to the News-Sentinel's coverage of the Vols. They are Executive Sports Editor Steve Ahillen, Deputy Sports Editor Phil Kaplan and the other writers and copy editors. They are John Battle, Mark Burgess, Chuck Cavalaris, Malcolm Dunn, Nick Gates, Bob Hodge, Roland Julian, Lisette Kaczka, Bill Luther, and Nico Van Thyn.

Last, but not least, a special thanks to Photo Editor Jack Kirkland and his staff, who gave us all of those wonderful images of the Vols' special season.

Harry Moskos
Editor
The Knoxville News-Sentinel

SCRIPPS HOWARD
"Give Light and the people will find their own way."

The Knoxville News-Sentinel

PUBLISHER: BRUCE HARTMANN
EDITOR: HARRY MOSKOS
EDITORIAL PAGE EDITOR: HOYT CANADY
MANAGING EDITOR: FRANK CAGLE
EXECUTIVE SPORTS EDITOR: STEVE AHILLEN
SPORTS EDITOR: JOHN ADAMS
DEPUTY SPORTS EDITOR: PHIL KAPLAN
DIRECTOR OF PHOTOGRAPHY: JACK KIRKLAND
DIRECTOR OF MARKETING: SHELBA MURPHY

The Commercial Appeal

EDITOR & PRESIDENT: ANGUS MCEACHRAN
VICE PRESIDENT & GENERAL MANAGER:
    RICHARD H. REMMERT
MANAGING EDITOR: HENRY A. STOKES
DEPUTY MANAGING EDITOR: OTIS L. SANFORD
EXECUTIVE SPORTS EDITOR: JOHN STAMM
SPORTS COLUMNIST: GEOFF CALKINS
DEPUTY SPORTS EDITOR: GARY ROBINSON
DIRECTOR OF MARKETING: ELENA CAIÑAS

RESEARCH ACKNOWLEDGEMENTS
Bud Ford, Haywood Harris, David Grim, Tom Mattingly and the staff at the University of Tennessee Athletics Media Relations Office, Allsport Photography USA and AP/Wide World Photos, who assisted in providing key photos for this book, and Jack Lail, Yvette Fragile, Jonathan Bell and Traci McDonell of The Knoxville News-Sentinel OnLine Publishing staff, who assisted me in finding all of The News-Sentinel's stories and stats in their archives.

Copyright ©1999 by The Knoxville News-Sentinel Co. and The Memphis Publishing Company. All rights reserved.

No part of this work covered by the copyright hereon may be reproduced or used in any form or by any means graphic, electronic, or mechanical, including photographing, recording, taping or in information storage and retrieval systems without the permission of the publisher.

ISBN   0-9660788-7-X (Hardcover)
           0-9660788-4-5 (Softcover)

Produced by Epic Sports, Birmingham, Ala.
Cover Design by Tim Oliver, Shelton, CT. Email: mtoliver@worldnet.att.net
Book Design by Tim Oliver, Shelton, CT,
and Chris Kozlowski, Boston. Email: ckoz@adelphia.net
Title page illustration by Ron Morecraft.
Email: morecraftstudio@att.net
Photo Imaging by John Meyer, New York.

Typefaces: Bigblox, Palatino

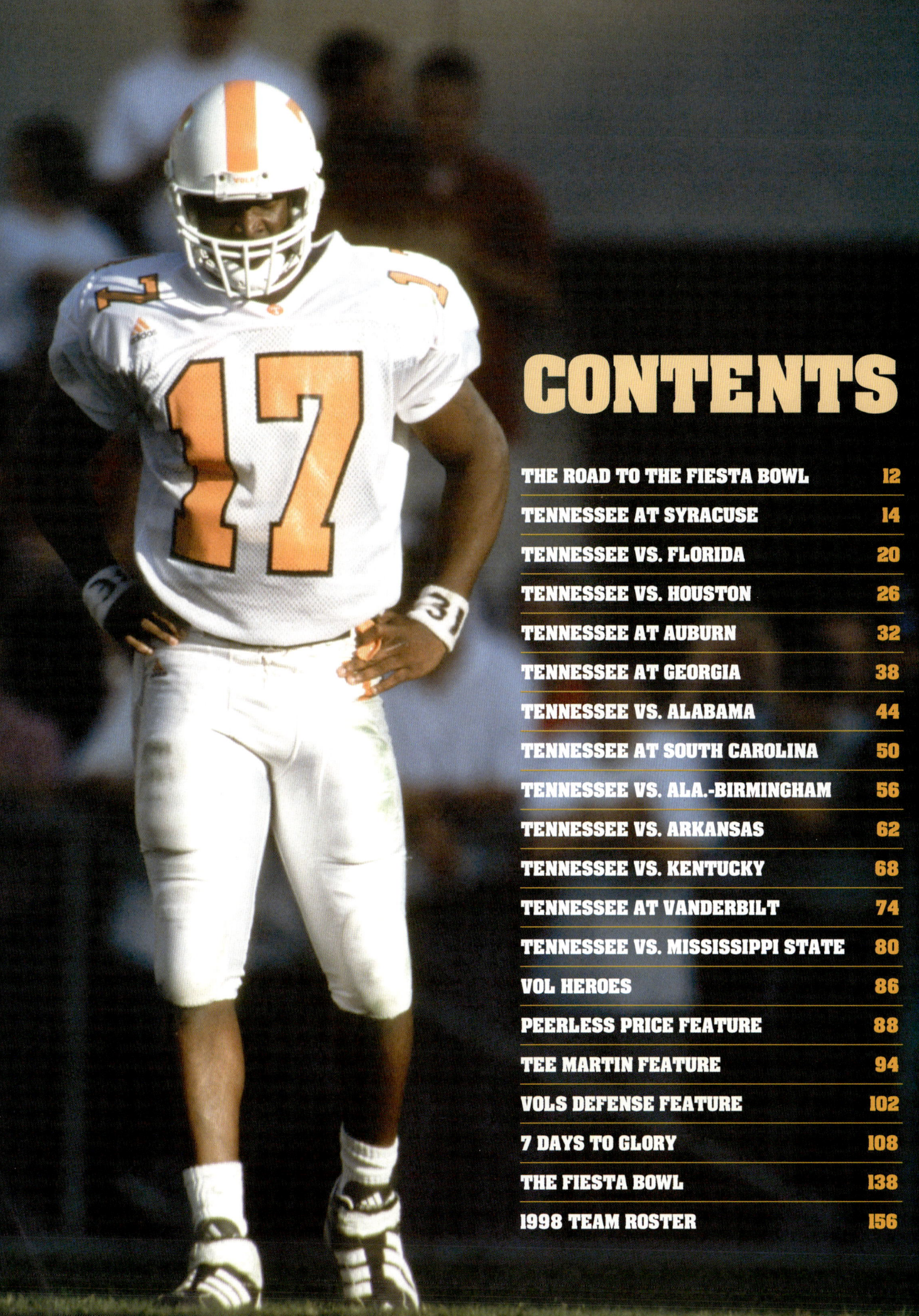

CONTENTS

THE ROAD TO THE FIESTA BOWL	12
TENNESSEE AT SYRACUSE	14
TENNESSEE VS. FLORIDA	20
TENNESSEE VS. HOUSTON	26
TENNESSEE AT AUBURN	32
TENNESSEE AT GEORGIA	38
TENNESSEE VS. ALABAMA	44
TENNESSEE AT SOUTH CAROLINA	50
TENNESSEE VS. ALA.-BIRMINGHAM	56
TENNESSEE VS. ARKANSAS	62
TENNESSEE VS. KENTUCKY	68
TENNESSEE AT VANDERBILT	74
TENNESSEE VS. MISSISSIPPI STATE	80
VOL HEROES	86
PEERLESS PRICE FEATURE	88
TEE MARTIN FEATURE	94
VOLS DEFENSE FEATURE	102
7 DAYS TO GLORY	108
THE FIESTA BOWL	138
1998 TEAM ROSTER	156

THE ROAD TO THE
FIESTA BOWL

DATE	OPPONENT	SCORE
Sept. 5	at Syracuse	34-33
Sept. 19	Florida	20-17 (OT)
Sept. 26	Houston	42-7
Oct. 3	at Auburn	17-9
Oct. 10	at Georgia	22-3
Oct. 24	Alabama	35-18
Oct. 31	at South Carolina	49-14
Nov. 7	Ala.-Birmingham	37-13
Nov. 14	Arkansas	28-24
Nov. 21	Kentucky	59-21
Nov. 28	at Vanderbilt	41-0

SEC CHAMPIONSHIP GAME

| Dec. 5 | Mississippi State | 24-14 |

The Road to No. 1

GAME 1
HALL KICKS FG IN FINAL SECONDS

| TENNESSEE | 34 |
| SYRACUSE | 33 |

SYRACUSE, N.Y., Sept. 5, 1998 — For weeks, the talk about this Orange Bowl in September centered on a new quarterback, a pair of Heisman Trophy candidates, a host of wonderful skill position players and a couple of suspect defenses.

True enough, they all shared the stage today at the Carrier Dome.

But at the end, it was Old Reliable who decided which shade of orange was a winner and which was a loser.

Senior co-captain Jeff Hall booted a 27-yard field goal as time ran out, lifting 10th-ranked Tennessee to a 34-33 victory over 17th-ranked Syracuse in a season opener that lived up to its billing.

It was the sixth score of a wild fourth quarter that wrung every drop of energy from the sellout crowd of 49,550, and kept a national ESPN audience enthralled to the end.

"It was down the middle," said Hall of the fateful boot, "but sometimes you have a little doubt.

"I took a little quick peek. I probably shouldn't have, but I wanted to."

Hall's kick culminated a 72-yard drive that sent the Vols' new quarterback, Tee Martin, home with a badly needed injection of confidence to face Florida in two weeks.

Martin was only 9-of-26 passing in his debut as successor to living legend Peyton Manning. And his

• **THE HEIR:** Tee Martin (17) only completed 7 of 26 passes but made the big plays when it counted.

Game 1: Tennessee at Syracuse

fumble with 5:25 to play set the stage for the Orangemen to take a 33-30 lead on Nate Trout's fourth field goal of the game with 2:38 to play.

"Tee made some mistakes and we knew he would," UT coach Phillip Fulmer said, "but I'm really proud of him.

"He stepped out of the shadow of Peyton today."

With the help of some power running by Jamal Lewis — 20 carries for 141 yards — and a drive-saving fourth-down pass interference flag against Syracuse, Martin moved the Vols into position for Hall to close the deal.

Martin's 17-yard completion to Peerless Price to the Syracuse 26 got Hall in range, and Lewis lugged it to the 10 in two more carries.

From there, Fulmer used his final time out to stop the clock with 4 seconds left. Hall, who kicked a game-winner against Georgia in the second game of his career, was ready.

"You'd be a fool to say there isn't any pressure," holder Benson Scott said, "but I always have total confidence in (snapper) Kevin (Ingram) and total confidence in Jeff.

"They were both on the money."

As the kick pierced the uprights, Tennessee's elation became Syracuse's deflation.

The Orangemen, led by brilliant senior quarterback Donovan McNabb, piled up 445 yards total offense and dominated the clock with 35 minutes, 31 seconds of possession time, compared to 24:29 for the Vols.

McNabb launched his Heisman campaign with 22-of-28 passing for 300 yards, including two touchdowns. He ran for 53 more, but three sacks reduced his net rushing to 17 yards.

"He's phenomenal," Fulmer said. "We may see another mobile quarterback, but I don't believe we'll see another one like that one."

In the fourth quarter, McNabb rallied the Orangemen from a 24-13 deficit by throwing a 17-yard TD strike to Kevin Johnson and running one in himself from the 6.

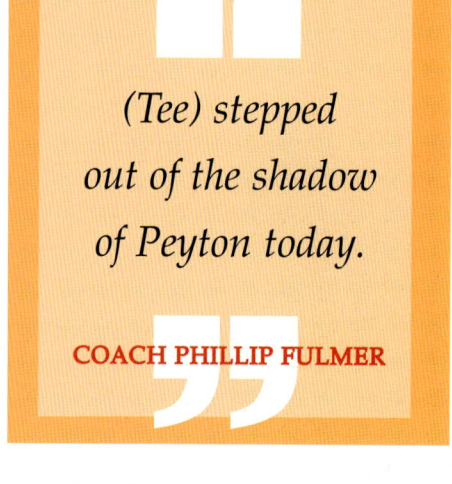

> *(Tee) stepped out of the shadow of Peyton today.*
>
> **COACH PHILLIP FULMER**

The latter made it 27-24 Syracuse with 9:49 left.

But there was more than one mobile quarterback under this roof.

Martin's 55-yard run on third-and-10 kept the Vols alive. Three plays later from the 8, he lobbed his second TD pass to Price.

"Just a great Tee Martin throw," Price said.

That nudged UT back on top, 31-27, with 8:29 left. However, with fatigue mounting for the Tennessee defense, it was a lead that wasn't likely to stand up.

It almost didn't stand up for 10 seconds.

On the ensuing kickoff, Kyle McIntosh broke through UT's coverage and was off to the races. The only man who could prevent a touchdown was Hall, the kicker.

He managed to grab onto McIntosh long enough to allow help to arrive and make the tackle at the Vols' 24.

"I'm not Al Wilson by any means," said Hall, "but at least we got him before he got to the end zone."

Hall's doggedness saved the Vols four points. The defense dug in and forced Syracuse to settle for a 41-yard Trout field goal.

Tennessee's 31-30 lead might have survived, but after two Lewis runs for a net 27 yards, Martin fumbled while looking to pass.

Syracuse pounced on UT's only turnover at its 41. On third-and-8, McNabb avoided Wilson's tackle and flung a 46-yard pass to Darryl Daniel at the Tennessee 11.

Once more, the defense, although bent, wouldn't break. Three runs left the Orangemen a yard short. On fourth-and-1 with 2:38 left, Trout's 19-yard field goal gave the home team a 33-31 advantage.

It wouldn't be enough.

Tennessee's final drive was reminiscent of its first.

After forcing a Syracuse punt on the game's opening possession, the Vols covered 80 yards in six plays.

● **AIRBORNE: Jamal Lewis powered over Syracuse for 141 yards and 1 TD.**

The Road to No. 1

Game 1: Tennessee at Syracuse

```
Tennessee   7   7   10   10  —  34
Syracuse    0  10    3   20  —  33
```

FIRST QUARTER
TENN — Price 12-yard reception from T. Martin (Jeff Hall kick), 6:38.

SECOND QUARTER
SYRA — Brominski 10-yard pass from Donovan McNabb (Nate Trout kick), 9:49.
TENN — Martin 1-yard run (Hall kick), :53.
SYRA — Trout 38-yard field goal, :00.

THIRD QUARTER
SYRA — Trout 20-yard field goal, 8:29.
TENN — Jamal Lewis 2-yard run (Hall kick), 5:28.
TENN — Hall 18-yard field goal, 3:15.

FOURTH QUARTER
SYRA — Johnson 17-yard reception from McNabb (McNabb conversion run failed), 12:13.
SYRA — McNabb 6-yard run (Kyle McIntosh conversion run), 9:49.
TENN — Price 8-yard pass from Martin (Hall kick), 8:29.
SYRA — Trout 41-yard field goal, 6:39.
SYRA — Trout 19 field goal, 2:38.
TENN — Hall 27-yard field goal, :00.
A-49-550.

GAME STATS

	TENN	SYRA
First Downs	18	23
Rushes-Yards	33-247	47-145
Passing Yards	143	300
Comp-Att-Int	9-26-0	22-28-0
Return Yards	125	165
Punts-Avg.	6-38.8	3-48.7
Fumbles-Lost	2-1	5-2
Penalties-Yards	3-20	8-79
Time of Possession	24:29	35:31

INDIVIDUAL STATS

RUSHING: Tennessee, Lewis 20-141, T. Martin 9-80, Bryson 2-21, Bartholomew 1-3, Henry 1-2. Syracuse, McIntosh 15-60, Konrad 10-48, Brown 4-18, McNabb 17-17, Johnson 2-2.

PASSING: Tennessee, T. Martin 9-26-0-143. Syracuse, McNabb 22-28-0-300.

RECEIVING: Tennessee, Price 6-87, Copeland 2-53, Bryson 1-3. Syracuse, Johnson 6-92, Spotwood 5-64, Konrad 5-63, Daniel 4-68, Brominski 1-10, Brown 1-3.

A 31-yard run by Lewis and a 33-yard Martin throw to Jeremaine Copeland preceded the 17-yard TD pass to Price.

However, before anyone got to wisecracking "Peyton who?" the Vols didn't make another first down until only three minutes remained in the first half.

After Syracuse tied it 7-7 on McNabb's 10-yard pass to tight end Steve Brominski, the Orangemen provided stuck-in-neutral Tennessee a shove.

Fullback Rob Konrad's fumble was recovered by Fred White at the Syracuse 14. Aided by a Syracuse penalty, Tennessee scored on a 1-yard sneak by Martin to go up, 14-7, with 53 seconds left in the half.

McNabb got three points back, hitting five consecutive passes to set up Trout's 38-yard field goal on the final play of the half.

The Orangemen, down 14-10, had a primo chance to go up in the third quarter, driving for a first down at UT's 5. But on third down, cornerback Dwayne Goodrich rode Konrad out of bounds at the 3 and Syracuse came away with only a 20-yard Trout field goal.

Tennessee padded its lead to 21-13 when Lewis scored on a 2-yard run. Momentum was there for the taking when McNabb fumbled and Jeff Coleman recovered at the Syracuse 29.

A 20-yard pass to Copeland reached the 9, but the Vols couldn't punch it in. Hall salvaged an 18-yard field goal to make it 24-13, and there things stood as the fourth-quarter fireworks began.

"The main thing I was looking for," Fulmer said, "was whether we won or lost, to show heart and fight and mental toughness and have a chance to go get better, because we're young in places.

"But we've got a chance to go get better and we got the win."

— *Mike Strange, The Knoxville News-Sentinel*

● **MEMORABLE:** Holder Benson Scott (10) gave thanks while his teammates celebrated Jeff Hall's winning field goal.

● **THE STREAK BEGINS:** Jeff Hall's game-winning kick would send the Vols on a 13-game win streak.

The Road to No. 1

VOLS END STREAK IN OVERTIME

GAME 2

TENNESSEE 20   FLORIDA 17   OT

• **UNFORGETTABLE:** The Vols' sideline erupted after defeating Florida, 20-17, in overtime in one of the greatest games ever played at Neyland Stadium.

KNOXVILLE, Sept. 19, 1998 — As Saturday night turned into Sunday morning, Tennessee fans wandered joyously, clutching clumps of sod or sprigs of hedge, souvenirs of their team's biggest football victory in years.

Inside the locker room under Neyland Stadium, the players and coaches clutched something better — their restored pride.

"I don't know who played good and who didn't play good, but we got the win," said head coach Phillip Fulmer after UT's 20-17 overtime victory over Florida.

"I don't know what monkey everybody's been talking about. I got that off my back."

Spencer Riley, the center who had been around for three of the five consecutive losses to the Gators, chomped a victory cigar.

The sting was gone from Fulmer's proclamation earlier in the week that UT's offensive line had been "totally embarrassed" last year in a 33-20 loss in Gainesville.

● **PERFECT OPENING:** Jamal Lewis (31), who rushed for 82 yards on 21 carries, sprints through a big gap in the Florida secondary.

Game 2: Tennessee vs. Florida

Florida	3	7	7	0	0	— 17
Tennessee	7	3	7	0	3	— 20

FIRST QUARTER
FLA — Cooper 21-yard field goal, 5.54.
TENN — Bryson 57-yard run (Hall kick), 4:52.

SECOND QUARTER
TENN — Hall 39-yard field goal, 7:12.
FLA — Taylor 8-yard pass from Palmer (Cooper kick), :20.

THIRD QUARTER
TENN — Price 29-yard pass from T. Martin (Hall kick), 7:36.
FLA — McGriff 70-yard pass (Chandler kick), 5:18.

FOURTH QUARTER
No scoring.

OVERTIME
TENN — Hall 41-yard field goal.
A-107,653.

GAME STATS

	FLA	TENN
First downs	17	17
Rushes-Yards	30-(-13)	34-171
Passing Yardage	409	64
Att-Comp-Int	31-49-1	7-20-1
Return Yards	115	96
Punts-Avg.	6-41.2	9-43.3
Fumbles-Lost	4-4	0-0
Penalties-Yards	9-65	8-78
Time of Possession	34:02	25:58

INDIVIDUAL STATS

RUSHING: Florida, Jackson 19-26, Taylor 1-6, Gillespie 1-3, Johnson 4-(-23), Palmer 5-(-25). Tennessee, Lewis 21-82, Bryson 5-64, T. Martin 8-25.

PASSING: Florida, Palmer 16-23-1-210, Johnson 15-26-0-199. Tennessee, T. Martin 7-20-1-64.

RECEIVING: Florida, McGriff 9-176, Taylor 8-80, D. Jackson 7-58, Gillespie 3-44, Karim 2-27, Edge 1-20, T. Jackson 1-4. Tennessee, Price 3-38, Bryson 2-9, Copeland 2-17.

"A lot of frustration was let off tonight," Riley said. "The offensive line had something to prove.

"A lot of people probably still don't think we did a good job, but Tee (Martin) was protected well for the most part. How many yards did we rush for?"

The answer was 171, about four times last year's total of 45.

"Thumbs up to our offensive line," Fulmer said. "It wasn't always pretty, but they got it done.

"They were able at least most of the time to neutralize an outstanding defensive front."

Riley was called for holding on third down of UT's overtime possession, forcing the Vols backward out of Jeff Hall's range.

On third-and-23 at the 38, Martin dropped back to throw, then scrambled 14 yards to the 24, well within reach of Hall's leg.

The Road to No. 1

● **CELEBRATION:** Cedrick Wilson (14) danced with Peerless Price (37) in the end zone after his third quarter touchdown catch.

"There was a pass called," Martin said. "I knew we had to get about 10 yards at least.

"Florida had their linebackers backed up, so I knew I had to scramble and get as much as I could."

When Hall trotted out, his teammates had supreme confidence in the senior who delivered the game-winning field goal at Syracuse two weeks ago as time expired.

"That kick right there, Jeff practices a hundred times a day," Riley said.

"I'd bet a hundred dollars ten times out of ten he makes that kick."

Hall did make it, and UT led, 20-17. Then it was up to the defense.

After Florida got one first down to the 15, the Vols successfully defended three passes, forcing the 32-yard field goal that Collins Cooper missed wide left.

"I was sitting there," Martin said, "knowing I had watched us come so close for so long. This feels so good.

"I knew they had missed the kick, so I started running across the field and shook hands with coach (Steve) Spurrier.

"He just looked shocked and said, 'Good game.'"

Fulmer wasn't shocked, he was overjoyed with the fight his team showed against its worst nightmare.

"You've got to give Florida credit," Fulmer said. "They battled right to the end — and even past the end.

"We did not turn the ball over and did not hurt ourselves. And the defense stepped up tonight, even though we left them on the field too long.

"I just can't say how proud I am of this football team and staff. I told them this is why you come to Tennessee, to play in games like this in this setting."

— *Mike Strange, The Knoxville News-Sentinel*

The Road to No. 1

GAME 3
MARTIN HITS 4 TD PASSES

| TENNESSEE | 42 |
| HOUSTON | 7 |

KNOXVILLE, Sept. 26, 1998 — As the final seconds ticked off tonight, placekicker Jeff Hall might have been counting the light bulbs atop Neyland Stadium.

He might have been on the bench studying for a marketing exam. He might have been on a cell phone ordering a pizza.

Whatever he was doing, he wasn't being asked to win a third consecutive game for fourth-ranked Tennessee.

No last-gasp theatrics this time. The Vols put their affairs in order early, sending Houston's Cougars back to Texas on the business end of a 42-7 spanking.

Having sidestepped a post-Florida hangover, Tennessee will take a 3-0 record on the road to Auburn next weekend.

"Our kids did a heckuva job of fighting through everybody patting them on the back last week, and wanting to talk to them about Auburn," Vols head coach Phillip Fulmer said.

"We didn't come out and play our best game tonight, but we played a pretty darn good one."

The Vols pleased a crowd of 106,447 by overwhelming Houston with 589 yards of offense.

The Cougars (0-4) hit town ranked No. 3 in the nation in stopping the run at 42.3 yards per game. Jamal Lewis eclipsed that on one carry, a 59-yard TD sprint in the third quarter.

He finished with 135 yards before yielding to

● **EYES ON THE BALL:** Peerless Price gathered in Tee Martin's 22-yard pass for a fourth-quarter TD.

Game 3: Tennessee vs. Houston

Travis Stephens and Travis Henry, who combined for another 131.

All told, Tennessee shredded the Cougars for 339 yards on the ground, a 7.9 average per attempt.

"I didn't see them playing anybody with good running backs like Tennessee has," Stephens said.

Tennessee had a good quarterback, too.

Tee Martin provided an effective complement through the air. He threw for four touchdowns, completed 14-of-19 attempts for 234 yards, all of which should improve his suspect season statistics by leaps and bounds.

"When you can do both, it keeps a defense on its toes," offensive tackle Chad Clifton said.

"They don't know where they're going to get hit from."

They even got hit from the unlikely 21-yard freshman passing combination of quarterback Burney Veazey to tight end John Finlayson to close the scoring.

Henry later had a 35-yard touchdown run wiped out by a holding penalty.

Houston's only score, a 19-yard pass from Jason McKinley to Scott Regimbauld, capped an 80-yard drive by the Cougars to open the second half.

A third-down personal-foul penalty against UT's defense — one of 11 flags on the Vols — kept the drive alive.

Martin's TD passes were 33 yards to Cedrick Wilson, 16 yards to Lewis, 63 yards to Shawn Bryson and 22 yards to Peerless Price.

Hall, the hero who decided UT's first two games with field goals on the final play at Syracuse and in overtime against Florida, passed a quiet night.

He tacked on an extra point here and there. His only field-goal try, a 48-yarder on the final snap of the first half, was blocked.

If there is a downside to the easy victory, it will be determined in the training room.

Star middle linebacker Al Wilson left the game in the first half with a separated shoulder. Bryson, the big-play fullback, suffered an ankle sprain.

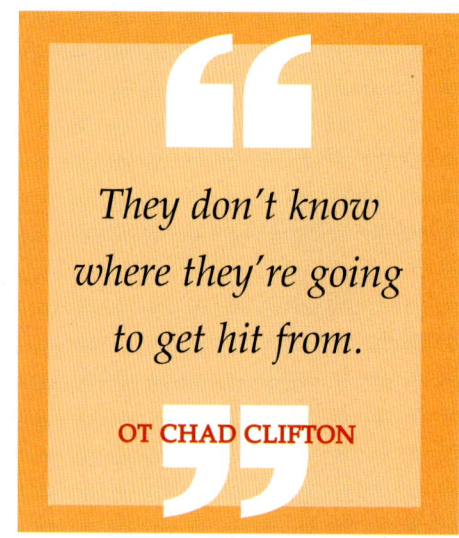

They don't know where they're going to get hit from.

OT CHAD CLIFTON

Offensive tackle Jarvis Reado went down early with a foot sprain and cornerback Steve Johnson (groin) watched the second half.

"I'm not sure anybody will be out for Auburn," Fulmer said, "but we've got a lot to do either to get them ready or get other people ready."

Whatever Martin's passing problems had been, they were quickly forgotten.

He threw touchdown passes on three of UT's first four possessions, although Lewis and Bryson deserved most of the credit for their footwork after the catches.

The other possession ended on Bryson's fumble — following an 11-yard pass reception from Martin.

By the time David Leaverton had to punt, the Vols led, 21-0.

Tennessee took the opening kickoff 72 yards in nine plays. Martin was 4-of-4 for 58 yards.

The payoff came on a 33-yard strike to Wilson.

"It was important we came out on that first drive and were machine-like," Fulmer said, "to let Houston know we were here to play."

The UT defense sent the same message, refusing to budge a yard on Houston's first possession.

The Cougars punted, but got the ball back on Bryson's fumble at their 35.

Houston moved into Tennessee territory, but punted again. This time, the Vols went 83 yards in 12 plays.

Stephens had a 30-yard run into Cougars' territory. Lewis returned in time to take a swing pass on the first play of the second quarter.

Price cleared the way, picking off two would-be tacklers at once, and Lewis motored 16 yards for the score to make it 14-0.

This time Houston drove into Tennessee territory, but Raynoch Thompson's sack on third-and-12 necessitated another Cougars' punt.

● **CAN'T CATCH ME: Jamal Lewis (31) raced past Houston defender Jason Parker for a 16-yard TD in the second quarter.**

Game 3: Tennessee vs. Houston

Lewis popped a 31-yard burst on first down, reaching midfield. Then the Vols went backward in 5-yard increments on three consecutive procedure penalties.

An animated Fulmer called time out and summoned the entire huddle to the sideline.

He evidently made his point. Two plays later, on second-and-25, Bryson caught a jump-screen pass from Martin on the left side and slashed back across the field until he found a corridor down the right sideline in front of the UT bench.

Feeding off blocks from Cosey Coleman and Eric Parker, Bryson completed the 63-yard touchdown play and the Vols led, 21-0, with 10:09 left in the half.

That's how it stayed. Houston punched as far as

The Road to No. 1

• **ELUSIVE:** Peerless Price (37), who had seven receptions for 76 yards and 1 TD, looks for an opening between a pair of Houston defenders.

the Tennessee 8, before Darwin Walker's sack of McKinley helped force a 35-yard field-goal try.

It sailed wide left with 22 seconds left in the half.

— *Mike Strange, The Knoxville News-Sentinel*

Houston	0	0	0	7	— 7
Tennessee	7	14	7	14	— 42

FIRST QUARTER

TENN — Wilson 33-yard pass from T. Martin (Hall kick), 9:33.

SECOND QUARTER

TENN — Lewis 16-yard pass from T. Martin (Hall kick), 14:52.
TENN — Bryson 63-yard pass from T. Martin (Hall kick), 10:09.

THIRD QUARTER

HOU — Regimbald 19-yard pass from McKinley (Waddell kick), 11:05.
TENN — Lewis 59-yard run (Hall kick), 7:36.

FOURTH QUARTER

TENN — Price 22-yard pass from T. Martin (Hall kick).
TENN — Finlayson 21-yard pass from Veazey (Hall kick).
A-106,417.

GAME STATS

	HOU	TENN
First downs	16	25
Rushes-Yards	31-39	43-334
Passing Yardage	200	255
Att-Comp-Int	21-31-0	15-20-1
Return Yards	64	72
Punts-Avg.	8-38.8	2-43.0
Fumbles-Lost	1-1	4-1
Penalties-Yards	8-62	11-95
Time of Possession	27:27	32:33

INDIVIDUAL STATS

RUSHING: Houston, Sanford 16-43, Penn 8-21, Baldwin 1-3, Green 2-(-2), Spencer 1-(-9), McKinley 3-(-17). Tennessee, Lewis 13-135, Henry 7-69, Stephens 9-62, T. Martin 6-63, Crosby 3-28, Bryson 1-19, Bartholomew 1-0, Veazey 2-(-3).

PASSING: Houston, McKinley 21-28-0-200, Helton 0-2-0-0, James 0-1-0-0. Tennessee, T. Martin 14-19-1-234, Veazey 1-1-0-21.

The Road to No. 1

GAME 4
DEFENSE TAKES TOUGH STAND

| TENNESSEE | 17 |
| AUBURN | 9 |

AUBURN, Ala., Oct. 3, 1998 — Whether it was long distance (90 yards) or close quarters (6 inches) Tennessee's defense delivered today.

Despite an offense reduced for all practical purposes to one Jamal Lewis touchdown, the No. 3 Vols made their return to Jordan-Hare Stadium a success, escaping with an improbable 17-9 victory over Auburn.

Tennessee scored 17 points in the first 13 minutes, then left the rest of the day up to a defensive unit that bent but would never break, even in the toughest of situations.

Offensively, it was a short highlight reel: a 67-yard touchdown run by Jamal Lewis on Tennessee's first snap of the day.

By then, the crowd of 85,214 was already rubbing its eyes in disbelief at the spectre of defensive end Shaun Ellis rambling 90 yards with an interception to give the Vols a 7-0 lead.

"It was a big surprise," said Ellis in the understatement of the year.

The defense contributed in more conventional ways, as well as Tennessee improved to 4-0, 2-0 in the SEC, in its first visit to Auburn since 1990.

Safety Derrick Edmonds recovered a fumble by

• **NOWHERE TO RUN:** Auburn quarterback Ben Leard (14) spent the afternoon trying to escape from the Vols' pass rush.

Game 4: Tennessee at Auburn

Auburn quarterback Ben Leard at the Tennessee 1 in the second quarter.

Two series later, after the Tigers had gotten on the scoreboard with a 40-yard Robert Bironas field goal, the Vols' defense was asked to perform the near-impossible.

Auburn sacked a back-pedaling Tee Martin and he fumbled toward the UT end zone. His old buddy from Mobile, Ala., defensive end Leonardo Carson, recovered not more 6 inches to a foot from the Tennessee goal line.

Three times, the Tigers punched forward, twice on sneaks by freshman quarterback Gabe Gross. Three times they were rebuffed by an unyielding wall of Vols.

On fourth-and-goal, linebacker Raynoch Thompson slashed in to nail fullback Tellie Embery in his tracks at the 2.

"That's got to be the greatest goal line stand I've ever been a part of or ever seen," said one of the ringleaders, Darwin Walker.

"I'm sure there have been some big ones in my 23 years (of coaching)," head coach Phillip Fulmer said, "but right now, that's the biggest one of all time."

The Tigers (1-3, 0-2 in the SEC) never got inside the 20 the rest of the way. Bironas added field goals of 44 and 45 yards in the second half.

Still, every Auburn possession of the second half penetrated into Tennessee territory. The final buzzer sounded with Gross flinging a pass toward Karsten Bailey in the end zone.

A posse of Vols defenders batted the ball to the ground and Tennessee had its first victory at Auburn since 1980 signed and sealed.

As the Vols headed home to prepare for another perilous trek, to Georgia on Saturday, they might be wondering what's wrong with their offense.

Martin was again off-target passing, hitting only 5-of-14 for 68 yards. Other than Lewis' TD sprint, the longest drive of the day was 39 yards.

David Leaverton punted seven times. Jeff Hall hit a 46-yard field goal in the first quarter, after missing wide on a 34-yard try.

Lewis toughed out 140 yards rushing.

"Today belonged to the defense," Fulmer said. "It's a team sport. I'm sure at some point in the season, the offense will pick up the defense."

Auburn was able to dent a UT defense ranked second nationally against the rush. The Tigers gained 181 yards on the ground, more than triple what the Vols' first three opponents averaged.

For a change, though, the Vols didn't get burned by the pass.

Auburn threw for 123 yards, 112 of that by Gross, a true freshman who came on when starter Ben Leard (1-of-10) suffered a bruised elbow.

"Tee didn't play very well," Fulmer said. "And if you're one-dimensional, which we were, kind of, today it's easier to stop you (running).

"But our defense playing so well did influence it (the game plan). We could see Auburn wasn't going to be able to score unless we helped them.

"I'm just tickled to death we got a win."

Auburn took the opening kickoff and unveiled an option package. Demontray Carter's 49-yard run would have scored had not Dwayne Goodrich been fast enough to run him down at the UT 11.

Then the Tigers decided to try their passing game. Big mistake.

After an incompletion, Leard backpedaled and attempted to underhand a shovel pass. He was hit by Corey Terry as he released and the wounded duck ended up in the arms of Ellis at the 10.

The big man lumbered toward the other end of the field. Auburn tailback Michael Burks caught up just past midfield, but couldn't get Ellis down.

On Ellis plodded, by now surrounded by a convoy of teammates, until he reached the end zone.

"It looked like he was praying for somebody to tackle him when he got to about the 30," said a grinning Walker.

> *Today belonged to the defense.*
> — COACH PHILLIP FULMER

● **END ZONE MEETING: Shawn Bryson (24) and Chad Clifton (67) hoisted halfback Jamal Lewis (31) after his 67-yard TD run in the first quarter.**

"But I knew he was going to get there because he had eight men beside him. That's the way we like to do it."

The next time the Vols touched the ball, the results were equally gratifying, if not quite so surprising.

After an Auburn punt, UT took over at its 33. Lewis burst up the middle, cut to the outside and outran the Tigers. The last man, defensive back Brad Ware, dived at the 10, but got only a shadow.

The 67-yard TD was the longest of Lewis' career and UT led, 14-0, just 4:19 into the game.

From there, the Vols' offense did little.

The defense did plenty. The goal-line stand surely will become a part of Tennessee football lore.

"We work on that every Monday," Fulmer said. "The kids have great technique and coach (Dan) Brooks does a great job coaching it."

— *Mike Strange, The Knoxville News-Sentinel*

Game 4: Tennessee at Auburn

• **ROAD BLOCK: The Vol defense stopped Tiger QB Gabe Gross (22) on the 1-yard line in the second quarter.**

The Road to No. 1

Tennessee	17	0	0	0 —	17
Auburn	0	3	3	3 —	9

FIRST QUARTER

TENN — Ellis 90-yard interception return (Hall kick), 12:32.
TENN — Lewis 67 yard run (Hall kick), 10:41.
TENN — Hall 46-yard field goal, 2:51.

SECOND QUARTER

AUB — Bironas 40-yard field goal, 7:39.

THIRD QUARTER

AUB — Bironas 44-yard field goal, 5:23.

FOURTH QUARTER

AUB. — Bironas 45-yard field goal, 14:55.
A-85,214.

GAME STATS

	TENN	AUB
First Downs	9	16
Rushes-Yards	36-150	46-181
Passing Yards	68	123
Comp-Att-Int	5-14-0	8-25-2
Return Yards	52	38
Punts-Avg.	7-37.4	6-40.8
Fumbles-Lost	3-2	2-1
Penalties-Yards	3-36	4-21
Time of Possession	26:43	33:17

INDIVIDUAL STATS

RUSHING: Tennessee, Lewis 18-140, Henry 6-13, Stephens 3-10, Bryson 2-3, Veazey 1-2, T.Martin 6-(-18). Auburn, Burks 26-82, Carter 4-70, Gross 9-25, Pennington 2-6, Leard 2-5, Embery 2-(-1), Team 1-(-6).

PASSING: Tennessee, T. Martin 5-14-0-68. Auburn, Gross 7-15-1-112, Leard 1-10-1-11.

RECEIVING: Tennessee, Copeland 2-55, Price 2-10, Bryson 1-3. Auburn, Bailey 2-33, Embrey 2-32, Robinson 2-23, Pennington 1-23, Lowe 1-12.

The Road to No. 1

GAME 5
VOLS DOMINATE DAWGS

| TENNESSEE | 22 |
| GEORGIA | 3 |

A THENS, Ga., Oct. 10, 1998 — Against all odds, Tennessee's march through Georgia continued today.

Instead of a march to the sea, it's beginning to look like a march to the desert.

The fourth-ranked Vols dominated No. 7 Georgia, 22-3, disappointing a crowd of 86,117, most of whom came to Sanford Stadium smelling Tennessee blood.

It was another stellar day for the UT defense, which hasn't allowed a touchdown in nine quarters.

The fact that the offense joined the party seriously bolsters the Vols' prospects down the road to the SEC championship game in Atlanta and, yes, even to the national championship Fiesta Bowl in Arizona.

"These kids aren't supposed to be this good, but they don't know that," said a proud head coach Phillip Fulmer, after making the rounds of kissing his three daughters and wife Vicky.

The win lifted the Vols to 5-0, 3-0 in the SEC, heading into an open date before Alabama visits Neyland Stadium on Oct. 24.

Georgia, a pregame favorite, fell to 4-1, 2-1 in the SEC, forced to swallow its eighth consecutive loss to its border rival from the north.

"That was a tough loss," said Georgia coach Jim Donnan. "They just whipped us."

In virtually every category. Consider, for instance, time of possession: 37:47 for the Vols, to 22:13 for the Bulldogs.

• **HIGH FLYING:** Travis Henry (20), who rushed for 53 yards on 16 carries, was one of two backs who replaced Jamal Lewis at halfback.

39

Game 5: Tennessee at Georgia

The Road to No. 1

Was star UT tailback Jamal Lewis really missing?

Yes, he was home recovering from season-ending knee surgery, but his teammates closed ranks.

Jeff Hall kicked three first-half field goals, from 27, 39 and 43 yards.

Travis Stephens rushed for 107 yards in his starting debut and Travis Henry added 53 more.

But the big story was quarterback Tee Martin.

After a rocky first half throwing two interceptions and fumbling on a sack in UT territory (teammate Spencer Riley recovered), Martin bounced back with a vengeance.

In a third quarter that was a Tennessee tour de force from start to finish, Martin guided a pair of scoring drives, culminating each with 3-yard touchdown passes.

The first came on a roll-out to Cedrick Wilson, polishing off a 65-yard drive with the second-half kickoff. Martin's 30-yard run was the big play.

It stayed 15-3, when UT was stopped on a two-point conversion run.

Three plays later, Dwayne Goodrich intercepted a deep ball from Georgia freshman quarterback phenom Quincy Carter — one of four Bulldog turnovers.

This time, Martin led the Vols 59 yards. He got the TD on third-and-goal from the 3, hitting Peerless Price, who dived under and around Bulldog defenders to the end zone.

Up 22-3 with 6:06 left in the third quarter, the Vols turned things back over to the defense, which was even better than in last weeks' 17-9 win at Auburn.

Martin was 7-of-9 passing in the second half, 16-of-26 for 156 yards on the day.

"The thing that impressed me," said offensive coordinator David Cutcliffe, "was he didn't let the two big mistakes turn into three, four or five.

"He handled the adversity well on the phone in the first half and we talked again at halftime.

"It was admirable how Tee Martin rallied himself and how his teammates stayed behind him."

Fulmer and Cutcliffe said they never considered shutting down the game plan after Martin's mistakes.

"Georgia's too good on offense," said Fulmer. "They have too much scoring ability."

• CAN'T HAVE IT: Cedrick Wilson (14), after making a reception, tries to prevent a Georgia defender from stripping the ball.

Game 5: Tennessee at Georgia

```
Tennessee   3   6   13   0   —   22
Georgia     3   0    0   0   —    3
```

FIRST QUARTER
TENN — Hall 27-yard field goal, 8:43.
GA — Hines 48-yard field goal, 1:55.

SECOND QUARTER
TENN — Hall 39-yard field goal, 3:16.
TENN — Hall 43-yard field goal, :07.

THIRD QUARTER
TENN — Wilson 3-yard from T. Martin (Martin conversion failed), 12:31.
TENN — Price 3-yard pass from T. Martin (Hall kick), 6:06.

FOURTH QUARTER
No scoring.
A-86,117.

GAME STATS

	TENN	GA
First Downs	21	14
Rushes-Yards	52-210	19-59
Passing Yards	156	195
Comp-Att-Int	16-26-2	14-38-3
Return Yards	5	64
Punts-Avg.	4-45.8	5-38.6
Fumbles-Lost	4-0	2-1
Penalties-Yards	8-61	10-91
Time of Possession	37:47	22:13

INDIVIDUAL STATS

RUSHING: Tennessee, Stephens 20-107, Henry 16-53, Stephens 3-10, T. Martin 15-45, Bryson 1-5. Georgia, Gary 6-45, Arnaud 4-21, Pass 1-1, Carter 7-(-3), Bradley 1-(-5).

PASSING: Tennessee, T. Martin 16-26-2-156. Georgia, Carter 14-37-2-195, Bailey 0-1-1-0.

RECEIVING: Tennessee, Price 5-35, Bryson 5-33, Wilson 4-63, Copeland 1-20, Finlayson 1-5. Georgia, Small 7-144, Bailey 3-21, Wiggins 1-11, Parker 1-8, Gary 1-6, Brown 1-5.

• **AERIAL MASTER: Tee Martin completed 16 of 26 passes for 156 yards and two TD's.**

And yet it produced only three points, on Hap Hines' 48-yard field goal.

The first half, in fact, boiled down to field-goal attempts, ending with UT on top, 9-3.

Tennessee tried three, made them all. Georgia hit one, missed one.

The first four snaps of the game included two turnovers deep in Bulldogs' territory, resulting in a stalemate.

Carter fumbled the second snap of the game and Tennessee's Deon Grant recovered at the Georgia 18.

The Vols' good fortune was squandered two plays later when Martin's pass was intercepted by Champ Bailey at the 3.

It was the only highlight for Georgia's two-way Heisman Trophy candidate.

Bailey didn't catch the first of his three receptions on offense until after the Vols were up, 22-3.

He also threw an interception to Grant when the Bulldogs tried to get tricky in the second half. On defense, he was victimized by Wilson's TD catch.

After forcing a Georgia punt, the Vols managed their second possession of the game better. A 16-yard scramble by Martin netted a first down at the 7.

That was as far as it got, though, and Hall kicked a 27-yarder.

Carter, the SEC player of the week after his big game at LSU last week, produced his first big play on third-and-21, heaving a 59-yard completion to Tony Small to the UT 15.

A personal foul on the Bulldogs, however, backed it up to the 30 and Georgia's momentum was snuffed. Hines got Georgia even at 3-3 with a field goal.

Tim Wansley picked off a second Martin pass at midfield early in the second quarter. Tennessee's defense again had all the answers and Hines eventually missed a 40-yard field goal try.

Hall showed him how.

A 34-yard completion from Martin to Wilson got Hall close enough for a 39-yard field goal, good for a 6-3 lead.

Thanks to more stout defense, Tennessee got another crack, taking a punt at its 34 with 1:31 left.

Rather than run out the clock, the Vols let Martin wing it. Two completions to Price reached the Georgia

26 and Hall hit from 43 with :05 on the clock.

The second half was all Tennessee. Smothering defense. A productive running game.

And, the return of the passing game.

"Tee," said Fulmer, "has got the ability to run and the ability to pass and he's got a good mind.

"But the best thing about Tee is his heart. He's got the heart of a lion.

"He's growing and he's going to keep getting better."

And so is Tennessee, with wins over its two biggest Eastern Division rivals in the bag.

"The Florida win (Sept. 19)," said Fulmer, "was only as good as we make it.

"At Auburn, we took a step and today at Georgia, we took a big step."

— Mike Strange, The Knoxville News-Sentinel

The Road to No. 1

GAME 6
FOURTH STRAIGHT WIN OVER TIDE

| TENNESSEE | 35 |
| ALABAMA | 18 |

KNOXVILLE, Oct. 24, 1998 — Peerless Price and his senior teammates now can go on to become grandparents and say they never lost to Alabama.

And Price can tell those grandkids how, in one glorious sprint the length of Neyland Stadium, he helped make that so.

Sparked by Price's timely 100-yard kickoff return for a touchdown, No. 3-ranked Tennessee put the hammer down on Alabama, 35-18, today, extending its domination over the Tide to four years.

The Vols, 6-0 for the first time since 1969, are hanging tough in the Bowl Championship Series scenario. At 4-0 in the SEC, they're in command of the Eastern Division race as they head to South Carolina next Saturday.

Tee Martin ran for two touchdowns, completed 10 of 14 passes, and handed off to Travis Henry who ran for two scores himself in a 113-yard rushing effort.

But back with 5:11 to play in the third quarter, the orange majority in the crowd of 107,289 — third largest in Neyland Stadium history — was a little nervous.

Shaun Alexander's 44-yard touchdown, the first allowed by UT's defense in 11 quarters, had just tightened the score. When Alabama (4-3, 3-3 in the SEC) got a 2-point conversion pass from quarterback Andrew Zow to Quincy Jackson, the difference was

• **SIDELINE DANCE: Peerless Price's 100-yard TD run in the third quarter silenced Alabama's hopes.**

• **IN THE TRENCHES:** Tennessee's defense wore down the Tide in the second half. It would be a trademark for the remainder of the season.

Game 6: Tennessee vs. Alabama

down to a field goal at 14-11.

"They scored, then got the two-point conversion. I knew momentum was kind of shifting their way," Price said.

"Coach (Phillip) Fulmer called us (the kickoff team) over and said, 'Let's get a good one.'"

Instead they got a great one.

Inserted today as a return man for the first time since a broken ankle in the spring of 1997, Price took the Alabama kickoff at the north goal line, broke through a wedge and found a path down the west sideline.

"Peerless blew down the Alabama sideline like a blur," said linebacker Raynoch Thompson, who watched from across the field.

Price did a good job staying in bounds, avoided the Alabama kicker and there was no stopping him.

The only concern was a flag that had been thrown early on. It was against Alabama for an illegal block below the waist.

"After everybody jumped on me, I saw the flag," Price said. "Then I saw everybody holding their breath, but thank God the flag was on them."

In the space of 20 seconds, Tennessee had padded its lead to 21-11 and reclaimed momentum.

"They ran it back so fast," Alexander said, "I didn't get a chance to sit down and get a drink of water."

After lightning struck, the thunder rolled in.

Less than two minutes later, Alabama was punting. The Vols took over at their 16 and drove 84 yards in 11 plays, all but one on the ground.

Henry scored on a 1-yard run, his ninth carry of the drive. With 12:56 to play, it was 28-11, and Alabama was done.

Done perhaps, but not willing to quit. Zow's 2-yard TD run with 6:14 left capped a 68-yard drive, most of it against Tennessee reserves.

"We put a whole bunch of second-teamers in there and they didn't respond very well," Fulmer said. "And Alabama, to their credit, wasn't about to quit."

The Tide forced a UT punt and got the ball back with 3:58 to play at the Tennessee 45.

The Vols wouldn't budge. On fourth-and-11, defensive end Corey Terry deflected Zow's pass into the sideline.

UT occupied the final 3:09 by driving for another touchdown.

● **HEAVY TRAFFIC:** Freshman fullback Will Bartholomew (45) pounds for 2 yards against Bama.

The Vols even converted a fourth-and-5 play with a 10-yard pass to Cedrick Wilson, one of only two pass attempts in the second half by Martin.

Henry bulled 5 yards for the score with 54 seconds to play.

The final horn sounded as Steve Johnson intercepted a deep ball from Zow, the game's only turnover.

A glance at the stats showed underdog Alabama virtually held its own in total yardage, 319 to UT's 348, and time of possession, 30:16 to Tennessee's 29:44.

But the Vols' ability to control the running game in the second half was telling.

"As the second quarter went on, we could tell they were getting tired," tackle Jarvis Reado said, "so we kept pounding on them."

But in the first half, Tennessee sent Martin out firing.

The Vols took the opening kickoff and raced 76 yards in seven plays. Martin's 22-yard hookup with Jeremaine Copeland was followed by a 16-yarder to Wilson into Alabama territory.

Travis Stephens got 15 on a run to the Alabama 19.

From there, Martin backed up and fired again to Wilson for 18 yards to the 1.

Martin got the score on a sneak and UT was on top, 7-0.

An exchange of punts swung field position in Alabama's favor. The Tide took over at the UT 34, Alexander bolted to the 23, but the Vols slammed the door.

Zow threw incomplete under a rush from Ron Green on third-and-11, and Ryan Pflugner's 41-yard field goal made it 7-3.

The Vols had a chance to get those three back, but Jeff Hall missed wide from 45 yards as the first quarter ended.

Another short David Leaverton punt gave the Tide decent field position and Zow — 18-of-39 for 177 yards — converted third-and-10 with a 16-yarder to Jackson.

The Alabama surge reached the UT 20, but Shaun Ellis dropped Alexander for a 3-yard loss. After an incompletion, Pflugner missed from 40 yards.

That set the stage for Tennessee's next scoring drive, 77 yards spread over 12 plays.

This time, it was almost all on the ground. Fulmer gambled on fourth-and-1 at his 45, but Phillip Crosby covered him, picking up the first down.

A 14-yard strike to Wilson moved the Vols into Alabama territory. Two plays later, Henry was hit in the backfield, but spun off a Reado block and raced 25 yards to the Alabama 6.

From the 5, Martin rolled left and hustled in for the score.

With a 14-3 lead, the Vols had 4:43 to protect it before halftime. Alabama made them work every second of it.

Zow converted three third downs with passes, but Pflugner missed from 47 yards as time expired.

Pflugner missed again, from 51 yards, on Alabama's first possession of the third quarter. When Tennessee's Hall followed suit with a 45-yard miss, the stage was set for Alexander's momentum-swinging touchdown.

But Price was there to swing it back.

"It's been a long time since anyone returned one around here," he said. "I'm just thankful it was me who had the opportunity."

— *Mike Strange, The Knoxville News-Sentinel*

Alabama 3 0 8 7 — 18
Tennessee 7 7 7 14 — 35

FIRST QUARTER
TENN — Martin 1-yard run (Hall kick), 12:48
ALA — Pflugner 41-yard field goal, 4:48

SECOND QUARTER
TENN — Martin 5-yard run (Hall kick), 4:43

THIRD QUARTER
ALA — Alexander 44-yard run (Q.Jackson pass from Zow), 5:11
TENN — Price 100-yard kickoff return (Hall kick), 4:51

FOURTH QUARTER
TENN — Henry 1-yard run (Hall kick), 12:56
ALA — Zow 2-yard run (Pflugner kick), 6:14
TENN — Henry 5-yard run (Hall kick), 00:54
A-107,289

GAME STATS

	ALA	TENN
First downs	21	22
Rushes-Yards	37-142	51-231
Passing Yardage	177	117
Comp-Att-Int	18-39-1	10-14-0
Return Yards	31	50
Punts-Avg.	4-49	4-36
Fumbles-Lost	3-0	1-0
Penalties-Yards	6-75	4-39
Time of Possession	30:16	29:44

INDIVIDUAL STATS

RUSHING: Alabama, Alexander 26-132, Locke 1-15, Richard 1-8, Zow 8-(minus 4), McClintock 1-(minus 9). Tennessee, Henry 22-113, Stephens 9-42, Martin 13-41, Bryson 2-16, Price 2-13, Crosby 2-4, Bartholomew 1-2.

PASSING: Alabama, Zow 18-39-1-177. Tennessee, Martin 10-14-0-117.

RECEIVING: Alabama, Q.Jackson 4-35, McClintock 3-34, Milons 2-34, Buchanan 2-25, Hall 2-21, Vaughn 2-14, Alexander 1-6, Bowens 1-5, Locke 1-3. Tennessee, Wilson 6-76, Copeland 1-22, Price 1-9, Henry 1-6, Bryson 1-4.

The Road to No. 1

GAME 7
MARTIN HITS FIRST 23 PASSES

TENNESSEE   49
SO. CAROLINA   14

COLUMBIA, S.C., Oct. 31, 1998 — Coaches like to say there are no easy wins in the SEC, especially on the road. Today was an exception.

Third-ranked Tennessee flattened hapless South Carolina, 49-14, at Williams-Brice Stadium and can now turn its thoughts to a momentous November.

A crowd that began as 69,523 gradually dissipated as South Carolina's long-shot upset hopes unraveled in the face of Tennessee's dominance.

It was the kind of day when:

■ Quarterback Tee Martin couldn't miss.

■ Tennessee's defense could get burned on third down, but still pitch a shutout into the fourth quarter.

■ Midway through the fourth quarter, the Tennessee assistant coaches could bail out of their press box booth and join the camaraderie on the sideline.

■ Finally, the nation, the pollsters and the Bowl Championship Series computer will have a lopsided victory by the Vols to digest.

"This shows we can put up a lot of points," fullback Shawn Bryson said, "and that we're one of the elite teams in America.

"It lets people know we're on our way to the top. If we take them one game at a time, we can get there."

● **PERFECT:** Tee Martin (17) set three NCAA records when he completed 23 of 24 passes for 315 yards and 4 TD's.

Game 7: Tennessee at South Carolina

The Vols are 7-0, 5-0 in the SEC, and headed home to take on Alabama-Birmingham, Arkansas and Kentucky one at a time.

"We control our own destiny," defensive end Shaun Ellis said.

As for South Carolina coach Brad Scott's destiny, stay tuned. The Gamecocks (1-8, 0-7 in the SEC) absorbed their eighth consecutive loss since opening day.

As it turned out, the Vols hardly needed a record-setting performance by Martin, but they got one.

He completed his first 23 passes — an NCAA single-game record — finishing 23-of-24 for 340 yards and four touchdowns.

Peerless Price had a pair of touchdowns among his 10 catches.

Jeremaine Copeland and Cedrick Wilson were on the business end of the other scoring passes.

Bryson, Phillip Crosby and Travis Henry scored on the ground.

Jeff Hall, along for the ride with seven conversion kicks, became the school career scoring leader.

The defense gave ground but no points, not until South Carolina was in a hopeless hole, trailing 42-0.

"Tennessee is a good football team," Scott said, "worthy of their national ranking.

"We had some opportunities in the first half, but they are too powerful a team to stay with for four quarters."

After watching his team roll up 561 yards, averaging 8.9 per play, UT coach Phillip Fulmer was only too happy to agree.

"We're not the greatest football team," he said, "but we're a pretty darn good football team."

Offensively, the Vols are gaining momentum, catching up with their defense.

UT hasn't committed a turnover in two consecutive games. The Vols scored three plays from the end of the first half and two plays into the third quarter to double a 14-0 lead to 28-0.

Both touchdowns were Martin-to-Price.

"South Carolina had certainly loaded up to stop the run," Fulmer said. "That left the passing game

● **HOT HANDS: Peerless Price (37) led UT receivers with 10 passes for 165 yards and two TD's.**

The Road to No. 1

Game 7: Tennessee at South Carolina

somewhat open."

Martin somewhat took advantage of it.

After South Carolina fumbled on its first possession of the game, Martin made it pay with a 21-yard TD strike to Copeland.

The Gamecocks fumbled on their second possession, Deon Grant recovering, but UT didn't score.

Then South Carolina missed a 39-yard field goal attempt. Four minutes later, Martin hit a wide-open Wilson for a 2-yard score and a 14-0 lead.

South Carolina had one more opportunity when it would have mattered. The Gamecocks drove to the UT 6 in the second quarter, but Chet Tucker's 23-yard field goal was blocked by Billy Ratliff.

"My hand is still stinging," Ratliff said a couple of hours later.

Martin's 15th consecutive completion hit Price just over the goal line for a 13-yard touchdown with 21 seconds left on the first-half clock.

His 18th consecutive completion came on the second play of the third quarter. It began innocently enough, a short pass to Price. But Price found a lane between Gamecocks and raced 71 yards to the end zone.

Bryson's 5-yard score made it 35-0 and the third quarter wasn't half over.

• **MAD DASH: South Carolina tailback Antoine Nesmith (40) rips for a first down against UT.**

The Gamecocks didn't record a first down in the second half until the third quarter was nearly over.

"The first half I don't think we played as well as we're capable of playing," UT defensive coordinator John Chavis said, "but that third quarter is what Tennessee's defense should be like."

Of course it's hard to get a first down when you don't have the ball. The Vols' next drive covered 11 plays.

It was noteworthy for including Martin's first and only incompletion, with 2:27 left in the third quarter.

If he was disappointed he didn't show it. Martin raced 30 yards to the 1, from where Crosby powered in to make it 42-0.

South Carolina's first score came on a Phil Petty pass of 24 yards to Zola Davis on fourth-and-12 with 11:39 to play.

Tennessee answered with Burney Veazey at quarterback, racing 61 yards in five plays.

Henry and Will Bartholomew had nice runs, then Veazey fired a 25-yard completion to David Martin at the 3. Two plays later, Henry surged in from the 1.

The Gamecocks took advantage of Tennessee's liberal substitutions, amassing an 18-play drive that delivered a 14-yard TD pass from Petty to Jermale Kelly with 4:01 to play.

"You've got to make a decision," Chavis said. "Are you worried about stats looking good, or do you want your team to continue to get better?

"The only way to get better is play them and that's what we chose to do."

— *Mike Strange, The Knoxville News-Sentinel*

```
Tennessee    7  14  21   7  —  49
S. Carolina  0   0   0  14  —  14
```

FIRST QUARTER
TENN — Copeland 21-yard pass from T. Martin (Hall kick), 10:03.

SECOND QUARTER
TENN — Wilson 2-yard pass from T. Martin (Hall kick), 9:27.
TENN — Price 13-yard pass from T. Martin (Hall kick), :15.

THIRD QUARTER
TENN — Price 71-yard pass from T. Martin (Hall kick), 14:01.
TENN — Bryson 5-yard run (Hall kick), 8:38.
TENN — Crosby 1-yard run (Hall kick), 1:14.

FOURTH QUARTER
SCAR — Davis 24-yard pass from Petty (Leavitt kick), 11:39.
TENN — Henry 1-yard rush (Hall kick), 9:26.
SCAR — Kelly 14-yard pass from Petty (Leavitt kick), 4:01.
A-69,523.

GAME STATS

	TENN	SC
First Downs	25	19
Rushes-Yards	38-221	33-87
Passing Yards	340	256
Comp-Att-Int	24-25-0	18-34-1
Return Yards	19	0
Punts-Avg.	1-28.0	2-47.5
Fumbles-Lost	0-0	3-2
Penalties-Yards	5-40	2-10
Time of Possession	31:11	28:49

INDIVIDUAL STATS

RUSHING: Tennessee, Henry 12-96, Stephens 13-48, T.Martin 4-37, Bartholomew 1-14, Veazey 2-12, Crosby 4-8, Bryson 2-6. South Carolina, Williams 11-63, Hambrick 10-17, Nesmith 5-4, Mixon 1-4, Petty 5-2, Wright 1-(minus 3).

PASSING: Tennessee, T. Martin 23-24-0-315, Veazey 1-1-0-25. South Carolina, Petty 11-21-0-147, Wright 7-13-1-109.

RECEIVING: Tennessee, Price 10-165, Copeland 6-74, Wilson 3-59, Henry 2-21, Stephens 1-(minus 2), D. Martin 1-25, B. Scott 1-(minus 2). South Carolina, Fleming 3-43, Kelly 3-63, Davis 3-54, Williams 3-30, Nesmith 2-19, Hambrick 2-22, Mays 1-16, Spikes 1-9.

The Road to No. 1

GAME 8
VOLS REACH NO. 1 RANKING

TENNESSEE	**37**
UAB	**13**

KNOXVILLE, Nov. 7, 1998 — The biggest cheer today in Neyland Stadium came at 7:05 p.m. — well after Tennessee had retired victorious to its locker room.

Maybe 2,000 Vols fans of the original 106,508 were still mingling in the chill when the public-address announcement revealed the shocker in Columbus — Michigan State 28, No. 1 Ohio State 24.

So there was joy in Big Orange Country after all, even on a homecoming afternoon when No. 2 UT was less than overwhelming in a 37-13 victory over Alabama-Birmingham.

By tomorrow, the Vols could be ranked No. 1 in the land for the first time since November, 1956.

"It's special to be considered in that mix," Tennessee head coach Phillip Fulmer said, "but there's so much football left to be played.

"It's up to us to remember how we got here."

As for Homecoming '98, the anticipated slaughter of a sacrificial lamb appeared to be gathering, but never quite materialized.

Three Tennessee turnovers not only robbed the Vols of scoring opportunities, but set up each of UAB's scores.

Three other times, UT had to settle for Jeff Hall field goals instead of touchdowns.

• **EXTRA YARDAGE: Peerless Price (37), who caught 6 passes for 103 yards, reaches for a first down against UAB.**

Game 8: Tennessee vs. Alabama-Birmingham

Missed tackles by Tennessee defensive reserves contributed heavily to the Blazers' only touchdown, a 32-yard run by backup quarterback Lee Jolly with 2:36 to play.

Still, the Vols are 8-0 for the first time since 1956. Next up is Arkansas, also 8-0 after shutting out Ole Miss, 34-0, today.

"Our focus now will be totally to get ready for Arkansas," Fulmer said, dismissing the possibility of poll-related distractions.

Travis Henry and Travis Stephens each had touchdown runs against UAB. Tee Martin ran for one score and threw 28 yards to Cedrick Wilson for the other touchdown.

UAB (2-7) got field goals of 20 and 36 yards from Rhett Gallego, prior to Jolly's touchdown — the first by the Blazers in five games against ranked opponents.

Martin's TD pass to Wilson with 12:05 left to play in the third quarter seemed to indicate the rout was on. That made it 31-3, and the Vols' defense was showing few if any cracks.

But Stephens lost the first of his two fumbles at the Tennessee 15. Even though UAB couldn't gain a yard, the Blazers still got a 36-yard field goal from Gallego to make it 31-6.

Next, the Vols overcame a dropped potential TD bomb by Shawn Bryson and drove for a first down at the UAB 7. However, Martin threw incomplete on third down from the 3, leaving it up to Hall to finish up.

His 20-yarder made it 34-6.

As the fourth quarter began, Tennessee again seemed to build momentum. The Blazers drove to the UT 18 only to see defensive end Shaun Ellis scoop up a fumble and motor 65 yards to the UAB 17.

Unfortunately for the Vols' offense, Elllis didn't close the deal the way he did on his interception at

- **UP HIGH: Cedrick Wilson (14) pulls down a first quarter pass over UAB defender Youdon Biassou.**

Auburn last month. Martin couldn't hit, then couldn't even find a receiver. Hall again had to kick the field goal.

His 37-yarder made it 37-6 with 10:29. That was still plenty of time to pour it on, but the Vols couldn't.

Stephens lost another fumble with 4:56 to play at the UAB 22.

The Blazers capitalized on spotty tackling by UT reserves to spring a couple of big plays and find the end zone.

Lucious Foster broke a tackle for a 39-yard gain into Tennessee territory. Three plays later, Jolly, who replaced shaken-up starter Daniel Dixon, faked a handoff to the fullback, broke free and scored from 32 yards out.

The Vols outgained UAB, 447 yards to 282, but the final margin wasn't what they had in mind.

"You've got to give UAB credit first," Fulmer said. "They played hard and ran the ball like they had to and shortened the game as much as they could."

The Blazers outgained the Vols on the ground, 211-173. That more than doubled the 91.4 rushing yards Tennessee had been allowing.

Martin was 18-of-25 passing for 274 yards.

Tennessee scored on four of its first five possessions of the game and led, 24-3, at the half.

The offense's first mistake was Martin losing a fumble near midfield that UAB was able to drive into field-goal range.

The Blazers almost made it within touchdown range. Fullback Cory Conley blasted 13 yards and then 15 on consecutive runs for a first-and-goal at the 9.

Conley's next three efforts were for zero, 4, and 2 yards. On fourth down at the 3, Gallego kicked a 20-yard field goal with 12:34 left in the half.

That cut Tennessee's lead to 10-3, but was only a temporary delay in the Vols' scoring parade.

The first play of the game was good for 39 yards — a 25-yard Stephens run with a 15-yard face-mask flag tacked on.

> "Our focus now will be totally to get ready for Arkansas.
>
> **COACH PHILLIP FULMER**

Game 8: Tennessee vs. Alabama-Birmingham

```
UAB          0   3   3   7  —  13
Tennessee   10  14  10   3  —  37
```

FIRST QUARTER

TENN — Hall 39-yard field goal, 13:18.
TENN — Henry 18-yard run (Hall kick), 4:36.

SECOND QUARTER

UAB — Gallego 20-yard field goal, 12:34.
TENN — Stephens 11-yard run (Hall kick), 9:29.
TENN — T. Martin 1-yard run (Hall kick), 4:26.

THIRD QUARTER

TENN — Wilson 28-yard pass from T. Martin (Hall kick), 12:05.
UAB — 36-yard field goal, 8:07.
TENN — Hall 20-yard field goal, 3:35.

FOURTH QUARTER

TENN — 37-yard field goal, 10:29.
UAB — Jolly 32-yard run (Gallego kick), 2:36.
A-106,508.

GAME STATS

	UAB	TENN
First downs	15	27
Rushes-Yards	51-211	43-173
Passing Yardage	71	274
Att-Comp-Int	7-14-0	18-25-0
Return Yards	177	72
Punts-Avg.	6-38.0	0-00.0
Fumbles-Lost	3-2	3-3
Penalties-Yards	7-43	4-30
Time of Possession	35:01	24:59

INDIVIDUAL STATS

RUSHING: UAB, Conley 16-39, Foster 12-83, Jolly 1-32, Coleman 1-7, Dixon 10-18, Morrow 1-7, Thatch 1-3, Miles 9-22. Tennessee, Henry 17-104, Stephens 14-61, Price 1-12, Crosby 3-3, Bartholomew 1-3, Bryson 1-1, T. Martin 6-(-11).

PASSING: UAB, Dixon 7-13-0-71, Jolly 0-1-0-0. Tennessee, T. Martin 18-25-0-274.

RECEIVING: UAB, Troupe 2-32, Malone 2-18, Foster 1-12, Ross 2-9. Tennessee, Price 6-103, Wilson 4-70, Copeland 4-60, Bryson 3-36, Stephens 1-5.

Martin hit Wilson for a first down at the UAB 24, but his quest for aerial perfection died there.

Two incompletions and a 3-yard run left fourth-and-7. Hall's 39-yard field goal was the consolation prize.

The Vols had to go a season-long 97 yards for their first touchdown, after the Blazers downed a punt at the 3.

Henry accounted for 54 of his 104 rushing yards during the drive on six carries. Six of the 10 plays were good for at least 11 yards. Henry cut outside to the right for an 18-yard TD run.

After Gallego's field goal, Tennessee got back on track with a 65-yard scoring drive.

Martin sneaked for a first down on fourth-and-1 at the UAB 20. This time it was Stephens' turn. He cut his touchdown run outside to the left and covered 11 yards.

That made it 17-3 with 9:29 left in the half.

Tennessee's defense pushed UAB backward to a fourth-and-19, and a 24-yard Blazers punt put the Vols in business only 46 yards from paydirt.

Martin-to-Wilson for 24 covered more than half the distance. After short connections with Bryson and Wilson again, Martin scored from the 1.

Down 24-3, with 4:26 left, UAB was able to grind out one first down, which was enough to keep the deficit from growing any more in the half.

— *Mike Strange, The Knoxville News-Sentinel*

• **DOUBLE TROUBLE:** Al Wilson (27) and Raynoch Thompson clown around for the fans after stopping UAB's attack.

The Road to No. 1

GAME 9
THE FUMBLE

| TENNESSEE | 28 |
| ARKANSAS | 24 |

• **BIG MOMENTS:** Peerless Price (37) celebrates his second quarter TD with Travis Henry (20) and Shawn Bryson. However, Hog quarterback Clint Stoerner's fourth quarter fumble put the Vols to rally to victory.

KNOXVILLE, Nov. 14, 1998 — Destiny? Fate? Luck?

Perhaps it was a combination of all three that helped the No. 1-ranked Tennessee Vols turn Neyland Stadium into a Nutt House today.

Tailback Travis Henry leaped one yard into the end zone with 28 seconds left to put an exclamation point on a 28-24 comeback victory over No. 10 Arkansas. Henry had 197 yards on 32 carries.

"Do you believe in miracles?" UT coach Phillip Fulmer was asked afterward.

"I believe in determination ... I believe in destiny perhaps," he answered.

The crowd of 106,365 had thinned slightly before the dramatic ending, but those who were left chanted "We're No. 1."

"That's the most incredible crowd I've ever been around in my life," Fulmer said.

The victory may not be enough to keep UT (9-0) atop both polls that are released tomorrow, but most importantly it keeps Fulmer's team in the hunt for a national championship.

Coach Houston Nutt's Razorbacks (8-1) seemingly had the game won when they took over at midfield leading, 24-21, with 1:54 remaining. However, on second down quarterback Clint Stoerner stumbled as he came away from center.

As Stoerner reach down with his right hand to regain his balance, the ball popped loose and UT's Billy Ratliff recovered at the Arkansas 43 with 1:43 left. Henry took over from there, gaining 15, 15, 11 and 1 yards to set up his dramatic winning TD dive.

Before the extra point, the Vols were penalized 15 yards for excessive celebration. Tee Martin got the snap and kneeled rather than risk Arkansas intercepting a pass and getting two points by returning it all the way.

"Somebody put pressure enough to make the quarterback trip and drop the ball,' Fulmer said, staying away from any suggestion his team was lucky on Stoerner's fumble.

Arkansas led the entire game until Henry's winning touchdown.

When the Razorbacks jumped ahead, 7-0, it was the first time the Vols trailed since a 3-0 deficit in the first quarter against Florida on Sept. 19.

Arkansas hurt UT all day by going to receiver Anthony Lucas against UT's shorter defensive backs. Lucas had 8 catches for 172 yards and two touchdowns.

His first TD catch gave the Hogs a 14-0 lead. His second padded the lead to 21-3. The Vols cut it to 21-10 just before the half on a 36-yard pass from Tee Martin to Peerless Price.

After an Arkansas field goal to open the third quarter, Tennessee drove 69 yards to cut Arkansas' lead to 24-17. Henry did most of the work, and Martin capped the drive by rolling out right and scrambling four yards into the end zone. It was only the third rushing touchdown against Arkansas in nine games.

On its next drive deep into Arkansas territory, perhaps Tennessee offensive coordinator David Cutcliffe remembered the derring-do in last year's Arkansas game when quarterback Peyton Manning caught a pass on a trick play to set up a TD. This time, Cutcliffe called a gadget play by lining up four receivers to the left, but instead Martin turned right and hit Peerless

The Road to No. 1

● **BIG SHOULDERS:** Travis Henry (20) carried all five plays on the Vols' 43-yard game-winning drive in the closing minutes.

Price for a 4-yard gain to the 4.

Jeff Hall came on to kick his second field goal, a 21-yarder, as the gap narrowed to 24-20 with 57 seconds remaining in the third quarter.

In the fourth quarter, Arkansas went back to Lucas three times on a drive that stalled at UT's 20. On Todd Latourette's 37-yard field goal attempt, Deon Grant came running from 10 yards back, timed his jump perfectly in the middle of the line and batted down the kick.

UT's Al Wilson scooped up the ball and returned it to the Arkansas 36. However, Arkansas' defense stiffened and forced a UT punt that was downed at the 1.

Arkansas ate up some time by driving 40 yards before having to punt. With 2:56 remaining, the ball was snapped far over the head of punter Chris Akin,

Arkansas   7 14   3   0 — **24**
Tennessee 0 10 10   8 — **28**

FIRST QUARTER
ARK — Smith 14-yard pass from Stoerner (Latourette, 5.24.

SECOND QUARTER
ARK — Lucas 61-yard pass from Stoerner (Latourette kick), 14:50.
TENN — Hall 41-yard field goal, 6:23.
ARK — Lucas 8-yard pass from Stoerner (Latourette kick), 3:15.
TENN — Price 36-yard pass from T. Martin (Hall kick), 2:03.

THIRD QUARTER
ARK — Latourette 33-yard field goal, 11:43.
TENN — T. Martin 4-yard run (Hall kick), 8:14.
TENN — Hall 21-yard field goal, :57.

FOURTH QUARTER
TENN — Safety, Ark. punter Akin kicks ball out of end zone after bad snap, 2:56.
TENN — Henry 1-yard run (conversion fails), :28.
A-106,365.

GAME STATS

	ARK	TENN
First downs	21	21
Rushes-Yards	41-81	45-222
Passing Yardage	274	155
Att-Comp-Int	17-34-1	10-27-1
Return Yards	77	140
Punts-Avg.	7-39.1	6-35.3
Fumbles-Lost	3-2	2-2
Penalties-Yards	7-62	9-75
Time of Possession	31:54	28:06

INDIVIDUAL STATS

RUSHING: Arkansas, Chukuma 18-97, Hill 16-20, Stoerner 6-5, Team 1-(-41). Tennessee, Lewis 21-82, Bryson 5-64, T. Martin 8-25.

PASSING: Arkansas, Stoerner 17-34-1-274. Tennessee, T. Martin 10-27-1-155.

RECEIVING: Arkansas, Lucas 8-172, Smith 4-73, Williams 2-5, Hill 2-5, Davenport 1-9. Tennessee, Price 5-59, Wilson 4-78, Copeland 1-18.

Game 9: Tennessee vs. Arkansas

who wisely chose to kick the ball through the end zone for a safety to make it 24-22.

It was the beginning of the late push that carried UT to victory.

Offensively, Arkansas' intentions were clear at the outset. The Razorbacks went right at UT cornerback Steve Johnson time and again.

And when Johnson wasn't in the game in the fourth quarter, the Razorbacks picked on his replacement, Andre Lott.

In the first half, Johnson gave up a 38-yard completion to flanker Michael Williams, a 62-yard TD pass to Lucas and missed a tackle near the line on a 32-yard run by Chris Chukwuma.

Arkansas also made no secret of its defensive scheme. On UT's first play, the Razorbacks put nine men within two yards of the line of scrimmage.

On UT's second possession, Arkansas put 10 men on the line and came with an all-out blitz on third down. Under heavy pressure, Martin hurried a pass that was nearly intercepted by Arkansas' Randy Garner. Arkansas nearly intercepted another Martin pass with five minutes left in the first quarter.

Martin's luck ran out early in the second quarter. Arkansas defensive end Carlos Hall pressured the Vols' quarterback, who threw a soft pass intended for Jeremaine Copeland that was intercepted.

While UT was struggling, the Razorbacks took advantage of critical mistakes on Vols' special teams, defense and offense.

UT's Tim Sewell found a hole on the line and nearly blocked an Akins punt. However, Sewell was called for roughing to keep the drive alive.

The loss of field position came back to haunt the Vols, who had to start their next drive at their 8. Travis Stephens, who had lost his starting job because of fumbling problems, coughed up the ball on second down and the Hogs took over at the 23.

Three runs by Madre Hill moved the ball to the 14, where Stoerner hit Emanuel Smith for a touchdown. Arkansas had a chance to extend its lead to 14-0, driving to UT's 8 late in the first quarter.

However, Grant ended the drive with an interception in the back of the end zone.

— Gary Lundy, *The Knoxville News-Sentinel*

• **MOMENT OF THANKS: After the wild finish against Arkansas, the Vols gathered for a brief prayer.**

The Road to No. 1

The Road to No. 1

GAME 10
VOLS STEAMROLL COUCH, CATS

TENNESSEE 59
KENTUCKY 21

KNOXVILLE, Nov. 21, 1998 — Tennessee got to No. 1 proving it can win by an inch. today, the Vols showed they can win by a mile, too.

Lucky? Fortunate? Not this week. Try ruthless. Try dominating.

A 59-21 rout of Kentucky before 107,252 at Neyland Stadium clinched a second consecutive SEC East title. After a visit to Vanderbilt, the Vols (10-0, 7-0 in the SEC) will play in the SEC Championship game on Dec. 5 in the Georgia Dome.

Tennessee made a mockery of the pregame analysis by matching the 59 points Peyton Manning & Co. hung on the Wildcats last year in Lexington.

The Vols' defense was a quantum leap better this year, holding Heisman Trophy candidate Tim Couch in check time and again.

The quarterback in the highlight clips this week will be Tee Martin.

Martin was 13-of-20 for 189 yards. He rifled a 55-yard scoring pass to Cedrick Wilson and ran 33 yards for another touchdown.

Jeff Hall kicked three field goals and scored 15 points to become the SEC's new career scoring leader.

Six different Vols found the end zone. Shawn Bryson did it twice, on a 1-yard run and a 58-yard sprint.

• **LONG DISTANCE:** With 3 Wildcat defenders in pursuit, Shawn Bryson (24) ran 58 yards for a second quarter TD.

Game 10: Tennessee vs. Kentucky

Phillip Crosby and Travis Stephens had 1-yard touchdowns and Travis Henry scored from the 2.

Tennessee put the game out of reach in the first half, scoring 32 unanswered points after Kentucky briefly claimed a 7-6 lead.

In extending its domination of the Cats to 14 consecutive years, Tennessee rolled up 466 yards and held Kentucky to a season-low 376.

The Wildcats finish 7-4, 4-4 in the SEC, and await the school's first bowl bid since 1993.

It was an unhappy ending to a tragic week for a team that has coped with a traffic accident that claimed the life of one player plus a lifelong friend of Couch's. Starting center Jason Watts, the driver, is hospitalized.

"That would probably be the easiest excuse," said Kentucky coach Hal Mumme. "They thumped us pretty good.

"You're not going to go against these great athletes with an emotionally spent team."

Couch had big numbers, but he's had better days. He was 35-of-56 for 337 yards passing, was sacked six times and intercepted once.

His only breakthrough when it mattered was a 3-yard TD toss to Lance Mickelsen in the first quarter.

Couch and Mickelsen hooked up on another 3-yard touchdown with 4:16 to play against Tennessee reserves, following David Johnson's interception of a Burney Veazey pass. That was UT's only turnover.

"We might have played our best game on defense today," said UT head coach Phillip Fulmer. "Against that style of offense, to hold 'em the way we did is a great effort.

"I think our defense was a little embarrassed from last year."

Last year, the Wildcats rang up 634 yards, most ever against a Tennessee defense.

The Vols had a good plan today and executed it, even with star linebacker Al Wilson in street clothes nursing injuries.

Tennessee frequently pressured Couch with a pass rush. Kentucky's longest completion was 26 yards.

From its opening possession, when Coach Hal Mumme ordered a fake punt — it failed — Kentucky kept the offensive pressure turned up.

Five times, the Wildcats gambled on fourth down. They only converted once. Kentucky managed a scant

Kentucky	7	0	7	7	— 21
Tennessee	14	24	14	7	— 59

FIRST QUARTER
TENN — Hall 27-yard field goal, 11:05.
TENN — Hall 32-yard field goal, 7:09.
KY — Mickelsen 3-yard pass from Couch (Hanson kick), 4:56.
TENN — Bryson 1-yard run (Bryson pass from T. Martin), 1:09.

SECOND QUARTER
TENN — Wilson 55-yard pass from T. Martin, (Hall kick), 12:11.
TENN — Bryson 58-yard run (Hall kick), 9:28.
TENN — Hall 47-yard field goal.
TENN — Crosby 1-yard run (Hall kick), :16.

THIRD QUARTER
KY — Homer 1-yard run (Hanson kick), 10:02.
TENN — Henry 2-yard run (Hall kick), 7:03.
TENN — Martin 33-yard run (Hall kick), 0:00.

FOURTH QUARTER
TENN — Stephens 1-yard run (Hall kick), 8:41.
KY — Mickeksen 3-yard pass from Couch (Hanson kick), 4:16.
A-107,252.

GAME STATS

	UK	TENN
First downs	21	21
Rushes-Yards	29-39	45-237
Passing Yardage	337	229
Att-Comp-Int	35-58-1	15-25-1
Return Yards	98	52
Punts-Avg.	3-36.3	3-37.0
Fumbles-Lost	1-0	1-0
Penalties-Yards	7-61	8-45
Time of Possession	30:57	29:03

INDIVIDUAL STATS

RUSHING: Kentucky, Homer 13-50, Johnson 3-11, White 4-7, Shanklin 1-5, Carter 1-2, Couch 7-(-36). Tennessee, Henry 15-67, Bryson 4-63, T. Martin 8-54, Stephens 11-42, Bartholomew 1-11, Crosby 2-3, Veazey 2-(-3), Graham 2-(-3).

PASSING: Kentucky, Couch 35-56-1-337. Tennessee, T. Martin 13-20-0-189, Veazey 2-5-1-40.

RECEIVING: Kentucky, Yeast 7-102, Robinson 7-74, McCord 6-60, Coleman 5-57, White 5-30, Mickelsen 3-7, Homer 2-9, Comstock 1-(-2). Tennessee, Wilson 4-100, Price 3-60, Bryson 2-74, Finlayson 2-21, Copeland 2-12, Bryson 2-(-4), D. Martin 1-29, Taylor 1-11.

The Road to No. 1

39 yards rushing, an ineffective complement to Couch.

Tennessee's offense was a picture of balance — 237 yards rushing and 229 passing. The Vols scored on 10 of 12 possessions before Fulmer called off the dogs.

Kentucky's defense opened with a three-and-out stop on Tennessee's first possession. And on the Vols' next two drives, they had to settle for Hall field goals instead of touchdowns, despite excellent field position.

Under the circumstances, a 6-0 Tennessee lead seemed a moral victory for the Wildcats. Surely, the Air Raid engines were revving to get off the ground.

Indeed, when Couch converted a third-and-9 with a 24-yard throw to Kevin Coleman, the Cats were off and flying.

The strikes started coming fast, 16, then 17, then 21 to the Vols' 3.

Couch got the score on a flip to Mickelsen and Kentucky led, 7-6, with 4:56 left in the first quarter.

Who knew that would be the Wildcats' high-water mark?

The Vols scored five touchdowns in their next six possessions, plus a 47-yard field goal from Hall.

Bryson went in standing up from the 1, capping a drive that included a one-handed catch by Peerless Price good for 41 yards.

Borrowing a page from Mumme's playbook, Fulmer got two points on a conversion pass from Martin to Bryson to make it 14-7.

Couch quickly had Kentucky on the march with five straight completions to the Vols' 25. Tennessee held its ground, though, forcing three incompletions, after which Seth Hanson missed a 42-yard field goal.

Martin showed his arm with a 55-yard TD bullet to Wilson, turning third-and-21 into six points.

Down 21-7, Kentucky couldn't move and punted. Three plays later, Bryson reprised his Florida touchdown, sprinting 58 yards to make it 28-7.

Tennessee then made Mumme pay for a fourth-down gamble when Darwin Walker sacked Couch for a 9-yard loss at the Kentucky 29.

Hall's field goal made it 31-7.

Mumme's disdain for the punt cost Kentucky again, this time in the form of an incompletion on fourth-and-2 at the Wildcats' 41. First-time starter Tad Golden broke up the pass.

With 4:15 left, Tennessee went into crunch mode, driving for a 1-yard Crosby touchdown with only 16 seconds left in the half.

• **WRAPPED UP:** Wildcats QB Tim Couch struggled against the Vol defense.

The Wildcats regrouped during intermission and drove for a first down at the UT 1. It took four tries before Derek Homer scooted in, barely getting the ball over the end zone pilon to make it 38-14.

The Vols hadn't lost their rhythm. Henry's 2-yard run capped a 62-yard drive.

Gerald Griffin's interception at midfield set the stage for Martin's 33-yard TD run to make it 52-14 on the final play of the third quarter.

Veazey guided the final score, a 45-yard drive that ended with Stephens leaping in on fourth down at the 1.

— *Mike Strange, The Knoxville News-Sentinel*

Game 10: Tennessee vs. Kentucky

● **LAST GRASP:** Travis Henry (20) was a difficult target for Kentucky defenders to haul down.

The Road to No. 1

The Road to No. 1

GAME 11
A PERFECT REGULAR SEASON

TENNESSEE 41
VANDERBILT 0

• **TOO MUCH:** Tee Martin (17) and Travis Henry (20) scored 3 TD's in the Vols' 41-0 rout over Vandy.

NASHVILLE, Nov. 28, 1998 — If such records are kept, it may have been the largest off-campus pep rally in Tennessee football history.

The No. 1-ranked Vols and their legions of admirers transformed Vanderbilt Stadium into a Big Orange fiesta today. There were a bunch of zeroes to celebrate.

■ The record: 11-0, for the first time since 1938.
■ The score: 41-0.
It should be enough for the poll voters. Will it be enough for the Bowl Championship Series computers?
■ The turnover ratio: 6-0.
What UT's offense couldn't generate, the defense could, forcing six Vanderbilt turnovers that were converted into 24 points.

A sellout crowd of 41,600 looked to the naked eye like 41,000 Tennessee fans and 600 Commodores diehards. The majority never experienced an anxious moment, unless you count a meager 3-0 lead after the first quarter.

A 17-point second quarter squelched any threat that Vandy (2-9, 1-7 in the SEC) would keep it uncomfortably close for the fourth consecutive year.

Next up, the Vols defend their SEC title on Saturday night in Atlanta against Western Division winner Mississippi State.

A win there and Tennessee hopes to be headed to the Fiesta Bowl to play for the national championship on Jan. 4.

"We're very flattered to be 11-0," UT defensive tackle Darwin Walker said, "but it's right back to

Game 11: Tennessee at Vanderbilt

● **DETERMINED:** Vol quarterback Tee Martin stretches for extra yardage after losing his helmet.

work on Sunday.

"We've got two games to go and they're probably the two biggest games this program's ever had."

Vanderbilt coach Woody Widenhofer is on the bandwagon.

"They're a well-deserving No. 1," he said. "In the four years that I've been here, this is the toughest team they've had."

Tennessee's 20-0 halftime lead became 27-0 on the second play of the third quarter when Chris Ramseur — filling in at middle linebacker for Al Wilson — returned a Commodores fumble for a touchdown.

Five of Vandy's seven second-half possessions ended in turnovers, which made it easy for the UT offense.

Tennessee's first shutout since 1995 against Southern Mississippi was never in jeopardy. Vanderbilt penetrated midfield only three times, reaching the UT 32 in the first half, the 28 in the second.

The Vols allowed only 174 yards, despite holding out Wilson and linebacker Raynoch Thompson, who was banged up last week against Kentucky.

Deon Grant, Fred White, Dwayne Goodrich and Derrick Edmonds had interceptions off Vanderbilt quarterback Greg Zolman, who was 12-of-31.

"I have to hand it to Tennessee's defense," Zolman said. "They're a great bunch of athletes.

"They're No. 1 outright and I wish them the best."

Ramseur's fumble recovery accounted for one touchdown. Walker's 26-yard return with another fumble set up UT's final score.

Tennessee's offense churned out 430 yards but wasn't flawless. David Leaverton was called on for six punts and a fourth-down conversion attempt failed.

A spectacular 67-yard touchdown play by Peerless Price after catching a short Tee Martin pass made it 10-0 in the second quarter.

Travis Henry's 12-yard TD run widened the margin to 17-0. Henry finished with 136 yards, his fourth 100-yard game since Jamal Lewis' season-ending knee injury.

Martin and Travis Stephens each had 1-yard touchdown runs in the second half.

Martin was 13-of-20 passing for 241 yards. His favorite target was no secret. Price had seven catches for a career-high 181 yards.

Jeff Hall added to his SEC career-leading scoring total with field goals of 22 and 42 yards, plus five extra points.

The Vols spent most of the first quarter getting the kinks out of Leaverton's punting leg. The only exception was when Hall's leg provided a 22-yard field goal.

A chop-block penalty snuffed the opening drive. The second one covered 90 yards, but that was 5 short of the end zone and the difference was four points.

After Martin was dropped on third-and-goal at the 5, Hall came on to make it 3-0.

As the second quarter began, the Commodores' offense finally shuddered to life. Vandy drove from its own 23 to the UT 32, but ended up punting.

Starting from their own 3, the Vols broke out on a 23-yard, third-down run by Henry.

Two plays later, Martin hit Price for a short gainer

Tennessee   3   17   7   14   —   41
Vanderbilt   0   0   0   0   —   0

FIRST QUARTER
TENN — Hall 22-yard field goal, 6:56.

SECOND QUARTER
TENN — Price 67-yard pass from Martin (Hall kick), 7:08.
TENN — Henry 12-yard run (Hall kick), 3:57.
TENN — Hall 42-yard field goal, .55.

THIRD QUARTER
TENN — Ramseur 10-yard fumble return (Hall kick), 14:04.

FOURTH QUARTER
TENN — Martin 1-yard run (Hall kick), 9:34.
TENN — Stephens 1-yard run (Hall kick), 6:34.
A–41,600.

GAME STATS

	TENN	VANDY
First Downs	17	11
Rushes-Yards	49-189	31-91
Passing Yards	241	83
Comp-Att-Int	13-20-0	12-31-4
Return Yards	40	74
Punts-Avg.	6-38.2	8-40.3
Fumbles-Lost	1-0	4-2
Penalties-Yards	5-48	4-20
Time of Possession	32:18	27:42

INDIVIDUAL STATS

RUSHING: Tennessee, Henry 22-136, Stephens 14-38, T.Martin 9-12, Crosby 2-7, Bryson 1-2, Veazey, 1-(-6). Vanderbilt, McGrath 18-65, Thomas 6-23, Zolman 6-2, Hogans 1-1.

PASSING: Tennessee, T. Martin 13-20-0-241. Vanderbilt, Zolman 12-31-4-83.

RECEIVING: Tennessee, Price 7-181, Wilson 4-50, D. Martin 1-5. Vanderbilt, Carson 2-2, Ditto 2-25, Hogans 2-10, Jones 1-25, Fleming 1-12, McGrath 1-9, Thomas 1-5, Robinson 1-(-5).

Game 11: Tennessee at Vanderbilt

The Road to No. 1

near the sideline. Price turned it into a long gainer, emerging from a pack of three Commodores and sprinting for a 67-yard score.

That made it 10-0, and after another Vanderbilt punt, Price almost set some kind of record for longest consecutive touchdown plays.

On first down from the UT 43, Martin faked an end-around handoff and fired deep. The ball hit Price in stride headed for the end zone, but he dropped it.

Tennessee didn't have to wait long to get another shot. Vanderbilt went three-and-out again and Jeremaine Copeland's 15-yard punt return reached the Vandy 48.

Henry blasted 36 yards to the 12, then 12 to the end zone and it was 17-0. Moments later, Grant finally got the first interception off Zolman.

Tennessee was only 31 yards from the kill shot, but didn't get it and Hall boomed a 42-yard field goal to make it 20-0 at the half.

Two plays after the second-half kickoff, Zolman hit Everett Robinson on a crossing route — but not nearly as hard as UT linebacker Eric Westmoreland hit Robinson.

The football popped loose, Ramseur scooped it up and motored into the end zone.

"That was the hit of the year in my book," an impressed Grant said.

One official signaled an incomplete pass, but after a huddle, the ruling was touchdown.

That made it 27-0, which was how the third quarter ended after UT failed to convert fourth down at the Vandy 25.

White's first career interception and 33-yard return set off the fourth-quarter scoring. Martin hit Cedrick Wilson for 18 yards, then 14, then scored on a 1-yard sneak with 9:34 to play.

The 34-0 lead quickly became 41-0.

On Vandy's third snap after the kickoff, Lew Thomas fumbled. Walker picked it up and was pushed out of bounds at the Commodores' 10 after a 26-yard return.

Stephens leaped over the pile from the 1, and with 6:34 left, the scoring was done.

— *Mike Strange, The Knoxville News-Sentinel*

• **PARTY TIME: Jeremaine Copeland (6) joined the Vols' sideline celebration in the game's final seconds.**

The Road to No. 1

GAME 12
VOLS WIN SEC CHAMPIONSHIP

TENNESSEE 24
MISS. STATE 14

ATLANTA, Dec. 5, 1998 — These SEC football titles don't come easy for Tennessee. But come they do.

On a day of upsets, the No. 1-ranked Vols survived Mississippi State's upset bid and kept their national championship hopes alive with a 24-14 victory in the SEC Championship Game at the Georgia Dome.

In a struggle reminiscent of last year's 30-29 championship game victory over Auburn, Tennessee had to come from behind in the fourth quarter, keeping a crowd of 74,795 in doubt.

It took a 41-yard touchdown pass from Tee Martin to Peerless Price with 6:15 to play to keep the dream alive.

That restored Tennessee to a 17-14 lead and 28 seconds later it was 24-14.

On the first snap after the kickoff following Price's touchdown, the Vols came roaring in and knocked the ball loose from Mississippi State quarterback Wayne Madkin.

Al Wilson got his hands on the ball, lost it and watched teammate Eric Westmoreland finally make the recovery at the Bulldogs' 26.

Martin went for the jugular and found it. On first down, he fired to a wide-open Cedrick Wilson for the touchdown.

● **MVP: Peerless Price scored the game-winning TD on a 41-yard pass from Tee Martin.**

Game 12: Tennessee vs. Mississippi State

With 5:47 left, it was 24-14. The Bulldogs were done.

Tennessee isn't. At 12-0, with its 13th SEC title, the Vols are headed to the Fiesta Bowl in Tempe, Ariz., to play for the national championship on Jan. 4.

Most likely the opponent will be Florida State.

Florida State jumped into the picture when UCLA and Kansas State — unbeaten along with the Vols going into today's games — suffered upset losses.

Tennessee's offense was stymied for more than 50 minutes, but its defense was nothing less than superb.

The Vols' de-fense didn't allow a point. The breakdowns came on offense and special teams.

Kevin Prentiss' 83-yard punt re-turn with 8:43 to play accounted for one score, the one that put State ahead, 14-10.

The Bulldogs' first TD was on a 70-yard interception return by cornerback Robert Bean in the first quarter.

Interceptions by Tennessee figured prominently as well.

Deon Grant's interception and 24-yard return set up for Tennessee's only first-half touchdown, a 2-yard dive by Travis Stephens.

With UT leading, 10-7, in the third quarter and both offenses struggling, Al Wilson, back in action after a two-game injury hiatus, made an interception that might well have buried the Bulldogs.

Wilson picked off a Madkin pass and raced 32 yards for an apparent touchdown that would have given the Vols a 16-7 lead.

However, the score was wiped off by an illegal block on the return.

The score stayed 10-7, Tennessee got the ball on the State 30 and two plays later Travis Henry fumbled. The Vols got nothing.

That's where it stayed until Prentiss got loose on his punt return and had Tennessee seemingly headed down a path to doom that had already been paved by UCLA and Kansas State.

But once again, Tennessee was resourceful on less than its best day. The dream lives on.

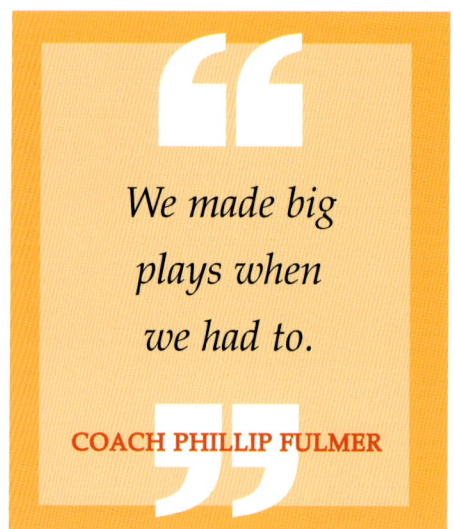

> *We made big plays when we had to.*
>
> **COACH PHILLIP FULMER**

The national ABC-TV audience stuck with the overtime Big 12 championship game didn't miss much from the Georgia Dome.

UT's David Leaverton and Mississippi State's Jeff Walker spent the first quarter swapping punts.

The one exception was the Bulldogs' second possession, which came up empty when Brian Hazelwood missed a 38-yard field goal try.

The two biggest plays of the first half were interceptions.

After a holding penalty, the Vols were backed up at their 18. Martin's third-and-12 heave for Price was picked off by Bean and the junior cornerback turned and surveyed the field.

He picked his way 70 yards, tiptoeing the last 20 down the sideline to the end zone. Flags were everywhere, but the touchdown stood.

The ABC-TV audience joined in to find Mississippi State on top, 7-0, with five seconds left in the first quarter.

Tennessee's response was Leaverton's third punt of the game.

However, three plays later, with Madkin throwing in the face of a fierce rush, Grant evened the interception score. His return 24 yards to the Bulldogs' 20 set up Tennessee's touchdown.

Stephens got 12 yards of it, the other 8 coming on a completion to Price for a first down at the 5.

From the 2, Stephens rode in behind the surge of Cosey Coleman, Shawn Bryson and Will Bartholomew.

Jeff Hall's PAT tied it 7-7 with 9:32 left in the half.

Aided by a personal foul on the Bulldogs, Tennessee's defense forced a punt and momentum was swinging the Vols' way.

Jeremaine Copeland took a Martin pass for 35 yards, his longest gainer of the year. On the next snap, Martin hit Price for 19 to the 8.

From there, things went awry, so Hall came on to nail a 31-yard field goal.

UT led, 10-7, with 5:09 on the clock, but the first-half scoring was over.

— *Mike Strange, The Knoxville News-Sentinel*

The Road to No. 1

● **BULLDOGGED:** State defender Anthony Derricks hauls down Jeremaine Copeland(6) after a reception.

Game 12: Tennessee vs. Mississippi State

● **CHAMPS:** The 24-14 win over the Bulldogs gave Tennessee its second straight SEC title.

The Road to No. 1

Miss. State 7 0 0 7 — 14
Tennessee 0 10 0 14 — 24

FIRST QUARTER
MSU — Bean 70-yard interception return (Hazelwood kick), 0:05

SECOND QUARTER
TENN — Stephens 2-yard run (Hall kick), 9:32
TENN — Hall 31-yard field goal, 5:09

THIRD QUARTER
No scoring.

FOURTH QUARTER
MSU — Prentiss 83 punt return (Hazelwood kick), 8:43
TENN — Price 41 pass from T. Martin (Hall kick), 6:15
TENN — Wilson 26 pass from T. Martin (Hall kick), 5:47
A-74,795.

GAME STATS

	MSU	TENN
First downs	9	21
Rushes-Yards	25-65	48-151
Passing Yards	84	208
Comp-Att-Int	10-25-2	15-33-1
Return Yards	222	45
Punts-Avg.	10-39.7	9-35.9
Fumbles-Lost	2-1	2-1
Penalties-Yards	10-100	4-30
Time of Possession	23:54	36:06

INDIVIDUAL STATS

RUSHING: Mississippi St., J.Johnson 14-38, Rainey 3-29, McKinley 1-1, Madkin 7-(minus 3). Tennessee, Henry 26-120, Stephens 12-50, Bartholomew 1-1, Martin 9-(minus 20).

PASSING: Mississippi St., Madkin 10-22-2-84, Morgan 0-3-0-0. Tennessee, Martin 15-32-1-208, Henry 0-1-0-0.

RECEIVING: Mississippi St., Cooper 5-44, Prentiss 2-27, J.Johnson 1-6, Kelly 1-4, Rainey 1-3. Tennessee, Price 6-97, Copeland 5-76, Wilson 2-27, Henry 1-4, Bryson 1-4.

The Heroes

The Heroes: Peerless Price

The Road to No. 1

Waiting For His
DAY IN THE SUN

By David Williams
The Commercial Appeal

There must be something in the air.

Well, of course there is: a football, sailing high and spiraling, and there's more where that came from.

And so they've come to catch it. They've come from all over, from throughout the South and from places more far-flung. They've come to the University of Tennessee over the years, caught passes by the scads and hundreds, and turned the place into Wide Receiver U.

Oh, there's something of a quarterback tradition hereabouts – the name Peyton Manning passes the lips first – but everybody knows the real action at UT has been at the other end of the forward pass.

Richmond Flowers. Stanley Morgan. Willie Gault. Tim McGee. Alvin Harper. Marcus Nash. Joey Kent. Carl Pickens.

The list, like all these fleet receivers, goes deep.

And after this dream season, it can go deeper still. We can add another name, and what a name it is: Peerless.

His full name is Peerless LeCross Price (more on that later) and he is one of them.

His name belongs with the Flowers and Morgans, the Gaults and McGees, the Harpers and Nashes and Kents, because his deeds do.

Here are the numbers: 151 catches for 2,497 yards and 21 touchdowns, all third in school history behind Kent and Nash.

But there's more to it than numbers. There's ingenuity, flair and timing. There's determination, dedication and a desire to do more than just get free, cradle a pass,

● **GAME-BREAKER: Peerless Price's stunning catches and electrifying runs often left opposing defenses in disarray.**

and find a soft place to fall.

"He makes as much happen, per touch, as any receiver we've ever had at Tennessee," head coach Phillip Fulmer has said.

But ask him about taking his place in that rare air occupied by all the Tennessee greats, and Price just

might balk – or beg some more time.

"I don't know if I do fit in, right now," he said. "Right now I can't say I fit in with those guys because those guys were great, and went on to have great professional careers.

"I know I broke a lot of their records and I'm right up there in the top two or three in every receiving category. But I don't know if I can fit in right now, because they went on to higher things after they left here."

A University of Tennessee football fan might tell Price that there's nothing higher than Volunteer football. And there's something to be said for that. When his game graces the NFL, he won't be cheered with such passion, or in such great numbers, as in his college days in Knoxville.

And even when he's gone, he won't be forgotten even if the Harpers and McGees – and Prices – of future seasons nudge him down the career receiving list.

They won't forget the name, nor the game.

They won't forget the struggle of his freshman season, when he was so discouraged about his lowly standing on the depth chart that he considered leaving.

They won't forget the great promise shown in his sophomore year. Or the leg injury he suffered in the 1997 Orange and White spring game, and how he surprised everyone by returning – even though he wasn't fully himself – in time for the start of his junior season.

They won't forget his senior season, when he became the biggest of the Vols' big-play threats, and helped lead them to the school's first undefeated regular season in 42 years, to a second straight Southeastern Conference championship, and to the national championship game.

"I'm going to throw it out there, Peerless. You have

• **LOTS OF BRASS:** The Vols' noted receiver was named MVP of the 1998 SEC and College National Championship games.

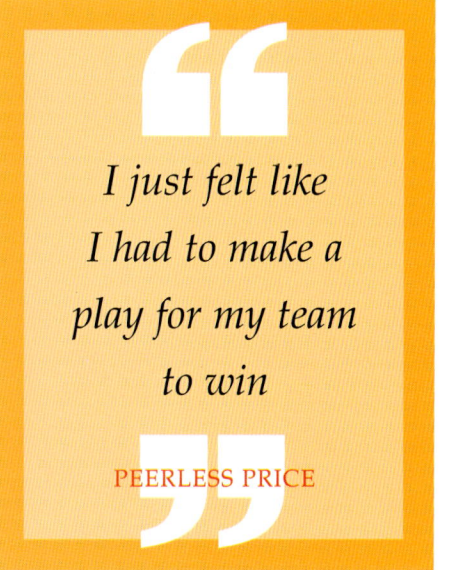

I just felt like I had to make a play for my team to win

PEERLESS PRICE

to go get it."

In some huddles, such words, spoken by a quarterback to his favorite receiver in the fading minutes of a game that was getting away, might have sounded like a prayer.

Here's guessing Tee Martin, the Vols quarterback, sounded like one more college student ordering a pizza.

So it is with Peerless Price, who in this remarkable season made the remarkable seem routine. There were one-handed grabs. There were leaping snags. There were so very many nifty moves after the catch.

And there was that Saturday night in the Georgia Dome when Martin placed his order and Price delivered, with the works.

This was in the SEC championship game, with a little more than six minutes to go and Mississippi State ahead, 14-10. Momentum had shifted. The game had taken on something of a maroon tint. The clock, it could be said, was running out on Tennessee's perfect season.

So Tee Martin looked at Peerless Price in the huddle and said what he said. Then he took the snap, dropped back, lofted the football high and long and awaited what must have seemed like the surest thing this side of gravity:

His favorite receiver, the end zone under him, plucking the ball from flight.

Peerless. Priceless.

Touchdown, Tennessee.

"I just felt like I had to make a play for my team to win," he said.

He seemed draped by a defender as he hauled he ball in, but didn't realize it at the time.

"I really didn't see him until I saw the replay," he said. "Then I realized how tough a catch it was. When I'm tuning in on the ball, that's all I'm tuning in on. I don't know where the DB is.

"He was real close. I think it was a great catch, great concentration. I think Tee threw a great ball where only I could catch it."

The Heroes: Peerless Price

For a wide receiver with visions of Sunday-afternoon passes floating into his sure hands, you might say the road, well, passes through Knoxville.

But there's a catch: There's great competition for playing time, and once on the field there only are so many balls to go around.

Put another way, you just can't show up from Dayton, Ohio, one day with the name Peerless and expect the world to fall at your fast feet.

Price arrived from Dayton with more than just the name, of course. He had credentials: player of the year for the city, a place on a couple of prep all-American teams. But he would have to wait his turn. Joey Kent and Marcus Nash were doing just fine as Peyton Manning's primary targets.

In the early days of his freshman season of 1995, he thought of leaving. How seriously?

"I was very serious, at first," he said, "he first couple of weeks when I felt like I should have been on the regular travel squad and I was on scout team. I was behind some guys I felt like I shouldn't have been behind.

"So I was very serious at first."

But the week of the Florida game, he was impressive enough impersonating the great Gator receivers that the coaches noticed.

"Coach Fulmer called me in his office and told me I was going to be on the travel squad," he said. "I went from fourth team to second team in a matter of a week."

The next game, against Mississippi State, he played his first game and caught his first pass, for 13 yards. It was a start.

For a hot-shot high school receiver, it's hard to resist a pass by Tennessee.

The Volunteers don't make many recruiting raids in Dayton, but Peerless Price knew all about Wide Receiver U. He knew the names and he knew the tradition. He told himself if he got the chance to play for UT, he'd leap for it.

"I knew of all the great ones," he said. "When you go on your recruiting visit, they put on the highlight tape and they show you guys. You're like, 'Wow. If they recruit me, maybe I'll be the next one in line.' "

Florida has itself a fine passing tradition, but Price said Gainesville was too far from home. Ohio State was too close, and, at the time, the Buckeyes ran the ball too much.

Happy how it turned out?

"Yeah," he said, "I'm pleased."

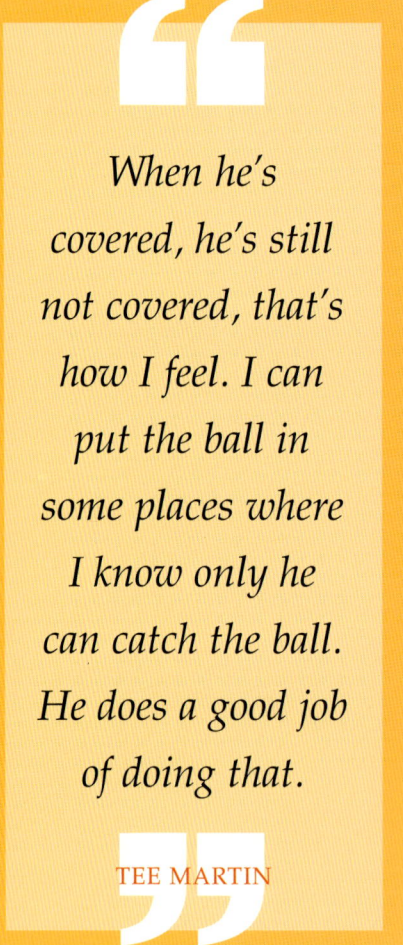

When he's covered, he's still not covered, that's how I feel. I can put the ball in some places where I know only he can catch the ball. He does a good job of doing that.

— TEE MARTIN

His senior season, the best of all, didn't begin that way.

It wasn't as tough as being stuck on the scout team as a freshman. It wasn't as rough as battling back from that leg injury before his junior season. But this was to be his breakout season, the season he emerged as the go-to guy, the star.

Trouble was, Peyton Manning was gone and the Vols offense was falling back to earth. The running game was being emphasized as Martin, a junior quarterback in his first season as a starter, was brought along slowly.

Martin completed nine passes in the season-opener against Syracuse. Nine passes – that was a good quarter for Manning. But Price caught six of them, two for touchdowns.

Next game, against Florida, Martin completed seven. Price caught three of those. Throughout the first half of the season, there were days when the Vol passing game hovered and floated more than it soared.

But when Martin emerged as a dangerous, accurate passer, there was a target waiting, and he was Peerless.

When Martin set an NCAA record by completing 23 straight passes against South Carolina, Price hauled in 10 of them for 165 yards and two touchdowns. He had 103 yards receiving the next game, against Alabama-

The Road to No. 1

● **RECORD BOOK: Peerless Price's 21 TD receptions ranks 3rd on the Vols' all-time record list.**

Birmingham. In the regular-season finale, he caught seven passes for 181 yards. Then came his six-catch, 97-yard performance in the SEC title game.

"When he's covered, he's still not covered, that's how I feel," Martin said. "I can put the ball in some places where I know only he can catch the ball. He does a good job of doing that.

"That's one of those intangibles that great receivers have. They know their quarterback. They know where to expect the football. That's kind of our relationship."

Ask Price about those early days of Martin's education, and the receiver said he always had faith in the quarterback.

"I had to," Price said with a smile, "or I would have gone to Coach Fulmer and told him I didn't want him to start."

Price, of course, does more than just pull long passes from the air. He takes short ones and turns them into long ones, eluding tackles, finding spaces and places, cracks and seams.

"That's a big part of my game," he said. "Against South Carolina, I caught a two-yard route and scored a 71-yard touchdown. Against Houston, I caught a five-yard route and took it for 31. Against Vanderbilt, I caught a five-yard route and took it 67.

"It's a part of the game every receiver wants, and every receiver wishes he has. But everybody doesn't."

Cedrick Wilson, poised to follow Price in the great line of UT wide receivers, said, "He means a lot to this team. He brings the speed, the excitement, the enthusiasm. He means a lot, just the catches that he makes and just the things that he does for this football team.

"I'm just a guy in the shadows. I'm the cleanup man."

Well, not everyone can be Peerless.

Yes, the name. You want to know about the name.

Well, there was a company called Peerless Trucking in Dayton, and his mother liked the sound of it. She liked the meaning, too, when she looked it up in the dictionary.

Young Peerless wasn't so crazy about it, though. Other kids made jokes about it. "I really thought it meant I didn't have any friends – without peers," he said.

But as he got older, as he began to have success in sports, he began to like the name. It looked good in the newspaper. He knew what it meant by now. He knew it was unique.

"It's different," he said. "It's not like Sean or something like that. When you've got a name like mine, it sticks out, people notice it."

But isn't a lot to live up to?

He shrugged and said, "If you know you're doing what can do to help your team, to help your family, as long as I'm pleasing my mom and she's happy for me ... I don't care what other folks say."

What anyone who's been paying attention through recent University of Tennessee football seasons would say is that Peerless Price's mother was not just inspired. She was prophetic.

The Heroes: Tee Martin

Tee
Made the Difference

By Mike Griffith
The Knoxville News-Sentinel

T he perfect season was almost over before it started.

Tee Martin trotted on the field and looked up at the clock: Two minutes, 27 seconds left. Tennessee was on its own 18-yard line trailing Syracuse, 33-31.

The 49,550 at the Carrier Dome roared, doing everything they could to rattle Martin, who had all of 16 passes worth of experience prior to this, the first start of his collegiate career.

Nervous? No, Martin said, he was *excited*. He had already brought the Vols back once in the fourth quarter. Martin lifted eyebrows with a 55-yard scramble through the Syracuse defense, and three plays later, he lofted a touchdown pass into the arms of his go-to receiver, Peerless Price, to give Tennessee a 31-27 lead.

The Orangemen's rally did no more to shake Martin than the boisterous New York crowd. Martin was anxious, chomping at the bit to show the Vols' fans there would be life after Peyton Manning, after all.

"I've been waiting for this game for two years," Martin said. "We had to make it. We had to score. It was time for me to step up."

Eight plays and 72 yards later, Martin turned the

●**MEDIA STAR:** Vols quarterback Tee Martin became the focus of most tv, radio and newspaper stories at the Fiesta Bowl.

The Heroes: Tee Martin

game over to All-Southeastern Conference kicker Jeff Hall at the Syracuse 10. Hall's 27-yarder split the uprights as time expired, giving Tennessee a 34-33 victory.

"That's when I knew he was going to be a great quarterback, on that last drive against Syracuse," said Vols' senior guard Mercedes Hamilton, one of four team captains. "He was so poised, like a general."

Tennessee tailback Jamal Lewis said he's never seen Martin any other way.

"Tee says a few things in the huddle now and then," Lewis said, "but really, he's not emotional out there. He just plays his game."

Larry Dickens laughed when remembering how much Taumarice Martin loved to play the games at the Boys and Girls Club in Mobile, Ala.

"I see him on television now, and he looks exactly like he did when he was a little boy," said Dickens, who has since moved to Mississippi and is the executive director of the Hattiesburg Salvation Army boys and girls club. "He started coming around when he was about 6. I thought baseball would be his ticket, he was dominant. He would always hit a home run and clear the bases. On defense, I had him at shortstop, where most of the balls were hit."

Martin also participated in tumbling, basketball and soccer. Football was one of the last sports he tried. He started out when he was 8 years old and played receiver. The quarterback position did not interest him.

"He wanted to be a running back and receiver," Dickens said. "I had to force him to play quarterback when we started calling plays. He was the only one who could remember all of them. We'd call a pass play and you could see his eyes go down to the ground. He wanted to run it all the time."

Martin smiled bashfully. "Yeah, that's right," he said. "I wanted to run over people. I grew up liking Jerry Rice and Walter Payton."

Martin's father, Pierre Maurice Marshall, was a teammate of Rice's for a year at Mississippi Valley State. His knees forced him to give up the sport. Like Tee, Pierre was a tremendous all-around athlete.

"I respect him because he taught me how to compete," Martin said. "I had to raise myself in many ways, but we still have a good relationship."

Martin moved around a great deal when he was young. By his count, he has held 23 different residences, shuffling between his mother, father, aunt, grandmother and great-grandmother. Tee, who is three years older than his brother, LaKendrick, and six years older than his sister, Shandrea, said there were benefits to staying with different relatives.

"It's like in high school where you have six periods and all different teachers," Martin said.

"You learn something different from all of them. I think it brought me and my brother and sister closer together because we met a lot of different people and learned a lot. We were smart kids, we understood my mother's situation. She was moving up, putting us in better situations. My mother worked hard for us our whole lives."

Marie Martin was 17 when she gave birth to Tamaurice Nigel Martin on July 25, 1978. Three years later, she married Marshall, but the two divorced soon after.

"Even when we were moving around, she saw us every day," Tee said. "My mother has always been my inspiration. She's achieved so much. Last year she got her college degree in nursing.

"All the females in my life made sure I stayed on my academics, and so did my uncle, Arthur Martin, he's an engineer," he said. "I couldn't go outside and play until I did my homework."

Marie remembers how Tee would play quietly in his room.

"He was always to himself," she said. "He would go in his room and draw pictures of cars and football play-

> *He wanted to be a running back and receiver. I had to force him to play quarterback when we started calling plays.*
>
> — LARRY DICKENS

ers. He loved his football."

Martin was out playing one day in Mobile's Luscher Park with LaKendrick and Shandrea when he met Henry Pough, then a young volunteer coach.

"He and his little sister and little brother were walking through the park and a ball got loose," said Pough, now 37 and working at DuPont. "He picked it up, and threw it back to us, a 30-yard spiral. My assistant coach and I just looked at each other."

Pough needed to convince Marie to let Tee play.

"She didn't want him to," he said. "She was afraid he'd get hurt, but he was big."

Big, strong and fast, Tee was special. He could throw the ball farther than anyone else, and he had a knack for understanding how the plays were supposed to work. But again, he wanted to play running back or receiver.

Again, his coach convinced him to play quarterback.

"By the time he was 11, he was doing things some high school quarterbacks couldn't," Pough said. "I had a playbook, and it was a thick one. He knew it back and forth, and I'd given him the liberty to change plays at the line. He actually knew the plays better than I did."

Pough was especially impressed with Martin's poise. Unlike the other children, Martin didn't argue, pout or fight.

"He was quiet, easy going," Pough said. "I was an in-your- face type of coach, real young and aggressive. I'd get aggravated and raise my voice. Tee just stared at me. It didn't faze him. He'd just look at me and say 'yes sir' or 'no sir.' "

Martin played for Pough and the Navco Vikings until he was 12. He and Pough are still close.

"We talk about a lot more than just football," Martin says. "He's like a father figure to me."

Pough would often pick Tee up and then drive him home after practice.

"He was living in a tough neighborhood, a bad area with heavy drugs and crime," Pough said. "I knew it was rough. Football was an outlet for him, and he looked forward to it every day."

Martin, like many others in urban areas, was forced to grow up quickly. He lost many high school classmates and friends to killings.

"You grieve, and you hurt," Martin said. "You go to class with someone, and the next day, they're not there. I was blessed with a great family, and I leaned on my parents, my brother, my sister and cousins. I was never tempted to go the wrong way in life."

Martin was the starting quarterback his freshman year at Mobile's Williamson High School. At the age of 14, Martin quarterbacked the Lions to an upset over senior Dameyune Craig and traditional high school power Blount. Craig, of course, went on to Auburn where he led the Tigers to their first SEC West title.

Beating Craig was just the beginning for Martin. Over his career, he passed for 4,054 yards and 36 touchdowns and ran for 1,035 yards and 13 touchdowns despite missing half his senior season because of

• **CLOSE CALL:** Early in the season, Tee Martin got pounded while developing his passing attack. By late October, opposing defenses would rarely get close to him.

injuries. Martin, who also played basketball and ran track, made all-state in football as a punter, averaging 43.3 yards per kick.

Martin wowed the coaches at Auburn when he went to their football camp after his sophomore season and threw the football 78 yards. He went to Alabama's football camp following his junior season and was just as impressive.

"I remember Tee very well, he was still Tamaurice then." said quarterback guru Homer Smith, then Alabama's offensive coordinator. "He was a top-flight quarterback prospect. He was smooth and athletic, and he had a tremendous desire to work. He liked to practice and take his repetitions."

Tennessee receivers coach Pat Washington had known about Martin long before either of the in-state schools. Washington, a Mobile native who played quarterback at Auburn, learned about Martin when he was still in middle school.

"I'd lived in the same neighborhood in the Maysville area of Mobile and played on the same park team when I was a kid," said Washington, who recruited Martin. "I knew his background, and I knew some people in his family. There was a connection there."

Martin was named Mobile County's Scholar Athlete of the Year his senior year at Williamson, but he wasn't as successful on the football field. The Lions went almost exclusively to the shotgun and the teams loaded up on Martin.

"The only running plays we had were quarterback draws," Martin said. He was sacked 11 times in the season opener, and later suffered an ankle injury that forced him to miss six games. Consequently, his senior statistics didn't compare to those he'd put up his junior year, when he was 115-of-258 for 2,074 yards and 21 touchdowns.

"It didn't matter to us what kind of senior year he had," Washington said. "I was impressed by his grades, and we'd based our scholarship offer on his junior year."

So had Nebraska, SMU, Notre Dame and Auburn. Martin had visions of himself at each of the schools. In the end, it came down to Auburn and Tennessee.

"Feelings didn't play into my decision," Martin said.

● **SILENT LEADER: Although soft-spoken, Tee Martin won the respect of his teammates with his steady play and lengthy film study.**

"I had to do what was best for me. I could have gone a lot of places and started my freshman or sophomore year, but I wanted to go to school and be in position to win a national championship. When I visited Tennessee, it just felt right.

"I wasn't an Alabama or Auburn fan, so that made it easier for me to go out of state."

Martin attempted only four passes his freshman year in Knoxville, but he was getting quality work in practice and absorbing the Vols' complex system.

Tennessee offensive coordinator Randy Sanders, then the running backs coach, went out of his way to encourage Martin. A former reserve quarterback himself, Sanders knew about the frustrations of being a backup.

"I just tried to learn as much as I could in those first two years so I could be ready," Martin said. "I had an understanding of what my role was."

Martin roomed with Manning on the road, learning how to be a quarterback off the field as well. Like Manning, Martin is very conscientious of how he represents himself and the university. He also acquired Manning's love of watching game film. While many of his teammates were playing video games or renting movies, Martin was watching game tapes.

Often, he'd put a tape in when he went to bed. "I'd wake up in the middle of the night and the screen would be blue," Martin said.

By the start of his sophomore year, Martin thought he was ready to take over as the Volunteers' starting quarterback. He, like many, believed Manning would forgo his senior season and enter the draft.

"I'm not sure if I was ready, but I felt I was," Martin said. "I was anxious to play and I wanted to play."

Martin played in five games and threw just 12 passes his sophomore year. The Tennessee coaches, mindful of the Heisman Trophy race, often left Manning under center until very late in the games. Martin's opportunities were limited.

The Vols enjoyed a fine season in 1997. Manning broke most all of the school's career passing marks and became the SEC's all-time leading passer. Manning injured his knee in the SEC Championship Game and was forced to sit out two weeks of Orange Bowl preparation, leaving Martin to work with the first team as the Vols readied for Nebraska.

"It was a transition phase," Martin said. "It gave the

The Heroes: Tee Martin

coaching staff a chance to see some of the things I could do."

Manning returned from the injury and played most all the game, but Martin had an opportunity to show his talents in the fourth quarter. Show out he did: Martin was 4-for-4 passing against the Cornhuskers for 53 yards, and he had an 11-yard run on the eight-play, 80-yard touchdown drive that closed the scoring in UT's 42-17 loss.

The next time Martin took the field, he did so as a leader.

"He came into the huddle the first day of spring practice, and he told us it was his team," Price said. "He told us to believe in him."

Five months later, in the come-from-behind win over Syracuse, Martin backed up his words.

Still, No. 2-ranked Florida was the next team on the schedule, and while the win over the Orangemen were impressive, not even Manning had managed to score a victory over the Gators. How could Martin, with only one collegiate start under his belt, be expected to do something that Manning couldn't and hadn't? In the two weeks preceding the Florida game, Martin was reminded that Tennessee had lost five straight to the Gators.

"I'm a different quarterback and this is a totally different team," Martin informed the skeptics. "We want to make our own identity. We're making our own names."

But what of Florida's aggressive, blitzing defense? Many felt Martin would be intimidated by what he'd seen on film.

"I laugh when people blitz me," Martin said. "We have so many weapon ... I'm sure they're sitting back scratching their heads in the defensive meeting rooms."

If they weren't before, they were after hearing how confidently Martin was approaching the game.

Tennessee's defense was just as confident, and senior middle linebacker Al Wilson helped keep the Vols in the game by forcing three fumbles. Meanwhile, Tennessee offensive coordinator David Cutcliffe was calling an ultra-conservative game. The offense was not being asked to win the game, so much as they were not to lose it.

But as the game moved to overtime, score tied 17-17, the script changed. Martin threw incomplete on first and second down from the Florida 25, and a third down run was wiped out by a holding penalty.

It was third-and-23 from the Florida 37. For the second consecutive Saturday, the game was on Martin's shoulders. For the second consecutive game, Martin stepped up in the clutch.

Martin took the snap and dropped back. Seeing that no receivers were open, he took off, sprinting up the center of the field. The Gators' defense couldn't close in on him until he'd gained 14 yards and put Tennessee in field goal range. Hall delivered a 41-yarder, and the Vols' defense took care of the rest.

"I stayed there at the stadium until 2 o'clock, it didn't really hit me until I went back onto the field," Martin said. "I woke up the next day and went to church at 11 o'clock."

Most Tennessee fans were thanking the heavens for Martin over the next two weeks, as the Vols improved to 4-0 with wins over Houston and Auburn. But a few were concerned with his numbers. The Tennessee sports information department had noted how Martin's 44-percent completion percentage through four games was the lowest at UT in 25 years.

"Tee throwing for 40 percent is not our goal," Cutcliffe said. "But there's so many things to look at beyond throwing the football."

Perhaps, but that's not how the oddsmakers saw it. Tennessee traveled to Georgia as an underdog. The Vols were undefeated, but they had lost Lewis to a knee injury in the Auburn game.

"We were leaning on our best offensive player, Jamal," Fulmer said. "Now we'll lean on our next best player, Tee."

Martin welcomed the challenge.

"There's going to be more pressure on the offense, and I'm the one coach will put more pressure on," Martin said. "I'm ready to step up."

Martin shook off a slow start against the Bulldogs and completed 7-of-9 passes for two touchdowns in the second half as the Vols pulled away for a surprisingly easy 22-3 victory.

Martin stayed hot over the next two games, victories over Alabama and South Carolina. Against the Gamecocks, he sizzled, setting NCAA records for consecutive completions and completion percentage in one game. Martin completed the first 23 passes he attempted in the 49-14 victory in Columbia, finishing 23-of-24 for 315 yards and four touchdowns.

The Road to No. 1

Martin's last play of the afternoon was to hand the game ball off to his mother.

"It was wonderful," said Marie, wearing a Tennessee jersey with her son's number 17 on it. "I'm glad he's getting his chance to show he's able to take Peyton Manning's place. The best is yet to come."

The Vols closed out the season with wins over UAB, Arkansas, Kentucky and Vanderbilt. Martin ranked 20th in the nation in passing efficiency as Tennessee headed to Atlanta's Georgia Dome, in search of its second consecutive SEC Championship.

Mississippi State, however, proved to be quite a hurdle. The Tennessee players were distracted by a midweek announcement that Cutcliffe was leaving to take the head coaching job at Ole Miss, and it showed. The Vols found themselves trailing the Bulldogs, 14-10, in the fourth quarter.

"We were playing like it was the first game of the season, not the 12th game," Martin said. "We had to pull together and score some points in a hurry."

Martin did just that. Dropping back from the MSU 41, he spotted Price racing down the sideline. The Mississippi State pass rush was coming hard, but Tee stepped up into the pocket anyway, and heaved a high-arcing pass into the end zone.

"I never saw the play," said Martin, who was knocked to the turf. "But I looked into the stands and saw them cheering, so I knew something good happened."

Price reeled in Martin's bomb, putting Tennessee out front. The Bulldogs fumbled on their first play after the ensuing kickoff. Martin came back on the field and put the game away on the very next play, looking off the safety and throwing back across the field to a wide-open Cedrick Wilson for a 26-yard touchdown. Two scores, 28 seconds, ball game.

Martin and the Vols learned they would play the Florida State Seminoles the next day. Florida State had the number one-ranked defense in the country, and a reputation for hitting quarterbacks.

But just as he'd laughed in the face of Florida's blitz, Martin came out smiling when asked about Bobby Bowden's Seminoles.

"I like this game, I like the sound of it and the feel of it," Martin said. "I like Florida State. I grew up a big fan of their program."

Once arriving in Tempe, Martin and his teammates spent more time answering questions about the favored Seminoles than themselves. The first question Martin was asked at media day was "What scares you about Florida State?"

Martin wrinkled his brow and shot an inquisitive look at the reported who asked the question.

"What scares us? Nothing scares us, they're not doing anything we can't handle," he said. "We've been tested in the running game, tested in the passing game. We were blitzed, zoned, you name it, we've seen it all."

Martin stayed particularly focused in the eight days of practice leading up to the Fiesta Bowl. His trademark smile was missing, and there was considerably more zip on his passes in practice.

"We had the attitude that we did going into the Syracuse game," Martin said. "We were mad and we wanted to prove we were better than people thought."

The Vols did just that, scoring a 23-16 victory over the Seminoles in the Fiesta Bowl to claim their first national championship since 1951.

"Tee has got to be the top quarterback that's come through Tennessee," said receiver Cedrick Wilson. "Not necessarily his stats, but you think about what he's done and nobody has done it before."

TEE MARTIN STATS

Comp-Att-Int	164-285-8
Passing Yards	2,442
Touchdowns	21
Yards Rushing	306
Touchdowns	7
Pass Efficiency	144.4

The Heroes: The Vol Defense

The Road to No. 1

Revenge of the Killer Cockroaches

By Gary Lundy
The Knoxville News-Sentinel

It would have been easy for Florida State coach Bobby Bowden to compare Tennessee's defense to the swarming bees that buzzed the Seminoles at practice in Arizona the week before the national championship game in the Fiesta Bowl.

No, too common. The nickname "Killer Bees" has been used in by both NFL and college teams.

Bowden chose to liken the Vols' defense to another insect.

"They're like cockroaches," Bowden said.

"They don't eat things. But they sure do mess things up."

The analogy isn't pretty, but it fits.

All season long, the Vols messed up opposing offenses with a unit that was more pesky than overpowering.

And like cockroaches, UT's defenders said they didn't get a lot of respect.

"The players were probably the only ones who believed we could do what we did," said cornerback Steve Johnson.

"I don't even think the coaches believed we could do what we did."

"We proved a lot of people wrong. Some people said we were a team of destiny or luck. But I think you need both."

Defensive coordinator John Chavis was the architect of the defense that will be remembered as one of the finest in school history.

The defense was built on three key elements: speed, pressure and the intense leadership of middle linebacker Al Wilson.

"I think Al is the best linebacker in college football without a doubt," defensive coordinator John Chavis said.

Added teammate Raynoch Thompson: "Our defense took on Al's personality.

"The team revolved around his attitude. Off the field, he's always laughing, but on the field I look at him sometimes and think, 'Man, what happened to you?' He's like Dr. Jekyll and Mr. Hyde."

"Al plays like a madman," Johnson said. "He's very emotional."

Told of his teammates' comments, Wilson responded matter-of-factly: "If I feel like something needs to be said, I'm going to say it. I feel like my teammates respect me enough to listen if I'm trying to get a point across."

Wilson didn't want to hear excuses.

He didn't want to hear about how Tennessee had to replace six defensive starters from 1997 — NFL draft picks Terry Fair, Leonard Little, Jonathan Brown and Cory Gaines, plus pro free-agent signees Bill Duff and Tori Noel.

Add to that the uncertain status of defensive linemen Shaun Ellis and Billy Ratliff. Ellis suffered a seri-

● **TOUGH GUY: Al Wilson, known for his jarring tackles and emotional play, is the leader of the Vol defense.**

The Heroes: The Vol Defense

ous hip injury in an auto accident last March.

Ratliff has bad knees and suffered temporary paralysis in a practice drill in 1997.

At the Fiesta Bowl media day, Thompson said the Vols' players appreciate their successes because they know how fortunate they are.

"Seeing Billy motionless on the ground that day almost gave me a heart attack," Thompson said. "We've just pulled together for each other."

Chavis recalled the day last April when he "walked in the huddle one day and other than linebacker Al Wilson, I was the tallest guy there. We had lost so many people from the year before and so many people out with injuries, I almost didn't know where I was.

"Nobody felt we would get very much done. Our players took that as a challenge."

Head coach Phillip Fulmer was criticized by many for promoting Chavis to defensive coordinator in 1995 because Chavis had never held that position at a Division I school. However, the last three years the Vols have ranked in the top three in total defense in the SEC, finishing second this season.

UT allowed only 94 yards rushing per game, sixth best in the nation. The Vols' defense finished the regular season strong, and didn't allow either Vanderbilt or Mississippi State to score a touchdown.

"When I was hired, I sat down with Coach Fulmer and we wanted to set our scheme to stop the running game," Chavis said.

"We felt like we had to build our defense with speed. When we are clicking, we are going to be able to do that. We got better and better every week.

Plus, we had very few breakdowns in communication and that's big.

"If you can get an offense in a one-dimensional situation, the advantage goes to the defense."

The emphasis on defensive speed factor was evident by the fact four UT linebackers were top running backs in high school.

Fulmer talked about Tennessee being a blue-collar team and it started with Chavis, the son of a sharecropper who drove a school bus in high school in South Carolina to help pay the family bills. It wasn't

• **SACK DOCTOR: John Chavis, the architect of Tennessee's stingy defense, discusses Fiesta Bowl strategy with his boss, Phillip Fulmer.**

unusual for him to work dawn to dark when the tobacco crop was being harvested.

"I'm only 5 feet, 8 inches tall and the tobacco would grow higher than I was," Chavis said. "So there was no air getting to me, no breeze. When it's 102 or 103 degrees, it's like being in an oven all day long."

Chavis learned to overcome adversity early in life, and that helped him endure some tough times as UT's defensive coordinator.

One of the low points was came when he was the butt of jokes after Florida scored 62 points against the Vols in his first season as coordinator in 1995.

"When you go back home after giving up 62 points, even your dog will try to bite you after that," he said with laugh.

In 1996, Chavis' defense led the SEC and had more talent than this national-championship unit. The '96 Vols held opponents to 237 yards per game, compared to 303 yards this season.

"As a coordinator there are games when it seems like you are on fire and can't make a bad call," Chavis said. "Then there are games when you struggle a little bit."

Chavis knows the perception of defenses are based more on wins and losses than yards allowed. In going unbeaten, UT defeated Florida for the first time since 1992. Defense carried the day and got the Vols over the hump.

"There was a lot of chemistry on this team," Chavis said. "This group on defense might not be as talented as the one two years ago, but I've never been around a team that accomplished more or had the chemistry that this team has."

There was no inkling of that chemistry in the opener against Syracuse.

The Vols gave up 445 yards of total offense to the Orangemen. Hampered by cramps that sent numerous defensive starters to the sidelines in the second half, UT was fortunate to pull out a 34-33 victory.

"If we had done a good job of tackling against Syracuse, it wouldn't have been close," Chavis said.

Cornerback Dwayne Goodrich said the team became accustomed to pulling out games in the fourth quarter.

"I think the Syracuse game prepared us for the Florida game, and that game prepared us for the

The Heroes: The Vol Defense

Arkansas game," Goodrich said. "The close games have been a plus for us. We were fortunate to win all of them."

After an open date, Tennessee's defense came back with a strong performance to hold Florida to minus 13 yards rushing in a 20-17 overtime victory.

Wilson caused a school-record three fumbles.

"He's dangerous at all times, but when Al gets really angry he comes up with a big play," Thompson said.

Fulmer said Wilson was as valuable to the Vols' defense this year as Peyton Manning was to the offense last year.

"I've never had a player who hits you as hard as Al does," Fulmer said.

Wilson led the Vols in big plays this year, including five caused fumbles and four sacks. He says boxing as a youngster helped bring out his aggressive nature.

"People have to look out for No. 27," said Thompson, who led the Vols in tackles. "Al got mad in the SEC Championship Game against Mississippi State and he just flew through a hole like he knew what the play was going to be."

Alabama-Birmingham coach Watson Brown called Wilson "the most incredible football player he'd ever seen."

His teammates say Wilson was so reckless and aggressive in practice they always kept one eye on the lookout to avoid getting run over by him as he pursued the ball carrier.

Hampered by a partially dislocated shoulder and a pulled groin, Wilson missed the Auburn, Kentucky and Vanderbilt games.

The cockroach analogy fits again. When one defensive player bit the dust, another came out of the woodwork.

"We haven't had to rely on one or two players," Chavis said.

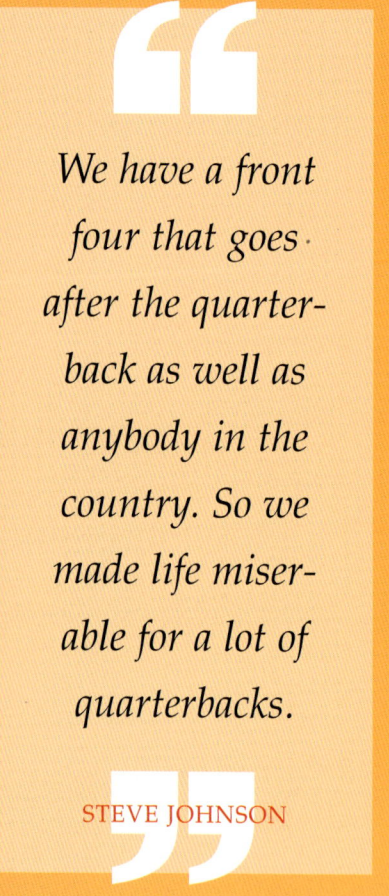

> *We have a front four that goes after the quarterback as well as anybody in the country. So we made life miserable for a lot of quarterbacks.*
>
> **STEVE JOHNSON**

"It's been somebody different each week."

Wilson sat out the Auburn game, and Westmoreland led the team with 11 tackles.

Perhaps the story that reveals the most about Westmoreland's intensity is what he did before facing Florida. Three days prior to the game, he suffered a serious ankle sprain in practice.

Chavis said 90 percent of players wouldn't have played because of the severity of the injury. However, Westmoreland spent an entire night in the training room to get ready, alternating ice and massage therapy every 30 minutes.

It worked. He played nearly every defensive snap in the victory. Westmoreland also had the hit of the year against Vanderbilt, causing a fumble that was returned for a touchdown. Because of Westmoreland's speed, Chavis describes him as "half safety and half linebacker."

"Eric has moved into the category of outstanding," Fulmer said before the Fiesta Bowl.

Ellis was another player with a knack for being in the right place at the right time. He returned a pass 90 yards for a touchdown against Auburn. He also picked up a fumble against Alabama Birmingham and returned it 65 yards.

"We have a front four that goes after the quarterback as well as anybody in the country," Johnson said. "So we made life miserable for a lot of quarterbacks."

Defensive end Corey Terry, a quiet player off the field, made a lot of noise rushing quarterbacks. Terry led the Vols with 15 quarterback pressures and tied Wilson with five caused fumbles. He ranked fifth on the team with 58 tackles.

Darwin Walker, a 292-pound defensive tackle, was the most dominant defensive lineman. He can bench press a team-high 535 pounds, and was often double-teamed.

Walker said the Vols stuck together on and off the field, which contributed to more of a team attitude than last year.

"You would hardly ever find a Tennessee player out in public by himself this season," Walker said.

"You'd usually find four or five of us together. In the past we had more stars. This is the most close-knit team I've ever been involved with."

Ratliff produced the most pivotal defensive play of the year in the fourth quarter of the Arkansas game. Ratliff charged off the ball into Arkansas' All-American Brandon Burlsworth, causing the offensive lineman to retreat into quarterback Clint Stoerner.

Stoerner tripped and fumbled, and Ratliff recovered, setting up the winning touchdown.

Ratliff and defensive tackle Ron Green were sometimes called "the golden boys" by their teammates because they were allowed to take a day or two off from practice each week during the season so they wouldn't further aggravate chronic knee pain.

Green — whose teammates nicknamed him "Freaky G" — showed up for the Fiesta Bowl with his hair dyed blond. Imagine somebody taking a chocolate Easter bunny and dipping the top of its head into a vat of yellow icing.

"It's like you're trying to be the Dennis Rodman of football," one of Green's relatives teased him.

The freshman who made the biggest impact on the team was defensive end Will Overstreet. He surprised himself on his first play of the Florida game by penetrating and knocking down quarterback Jesse Palmer as he released a pass.

Overstreet's playing time increased as the year progressed. He accounted for two of six UT sacks against Kentucky quarterback Tim Couch. It was the most times he had been sacked in his career.

Two other freshmen defenders also had big games against the Wildcats.

Defensive end Bernard Jackson recorded the first sack of his career, pulling Couch down from behind. Free safety Tad Golden got his first career start against Kentucky, and he made the most of it by making eight tackles.

Golden played behind starting sophomore free safety Deon Grant, who led the team with five interceptions. No interception was bigger than the one he made against Florida. Nafis Karim got behind the UT secondary and Jesse Palmer lofted the ball toward him midway in the fourth quarter.

Grant seemingly came out of nowhere and made a leaping one-hand interception to save a touchdown and the game.

"He kept us out of a lot of bad situations with the adjustments he made," Chavis said.

"It's good to have a guy who can cover form sideline to sideline to give help where it's needed.

"The Florida play was big. He had a play just as big against Georgia. There aren't a lot of safeties who have that kind of range."

Grant, who is 6-3, 205 pounds and has 40-inch vertical jump, also blocked a field goal against Arkansas. Teammate Antron Peebles recalled the time Grant was playing an intramural basketball game. Wilson threw an alley-oop pass and Peebles said it looked like Grant "was going to touch the top of the backboard."

Chavis said he knew Grant was going to be a good player from the moment he saw him make his first tackle in a college game.

"The first play he got in against UCLA in 1997, he hit (running back) Skip Hicks with one of the best licks I've ever seen and separated him from the football," Chavis said.

That ability of the defense to cause fumbles was a trademark of the '98 defense. Johnson said Chavis made it clear from the outset the Vols were going to be very aggressive on defense.

"He said if we didn't like getting in a receiver's face, or blitzing the quarterback, then we needed to transfer," Johnson said.

The players bought into the system and are fiercely loyal to Chavis. Thompson said it's like Chavis "invented" defense.

"I think the reason so many guys want to play for him is his aggressive style," strong safety Fred White said. "He puts us in the best situation possible and we just have to make the plays."

The defense's aggressiveness was reflected by the numbers. Tennessee caused 23 fumbles and recovered 19. The Vols had 31 sacks for minus 240 yards.

But for Chavis, Fulmer and the rest of the team these numbers were far more important than the rest: 13 wins, zero defeats.

And one national championship.

7 Days to Glory

Seven Days to Glory: December 28, 1998

Fiesta Has Glitz, Glamour

By Geoff Calkins
The Commercial Appeal

TEMPE, Ariz., Dec. 28, 1998 – Tennessee receiver Cedrick Wilson stood in the valley, looking out over the rugged brown mountains that circle this city, and thought about how he wound up in this place at this moment.

Had he ever been to Arizona?

"Oh, no."

Did he dare hope he would make it this year?

"Oh, no."

Could he think of any place he'd rather be this week?

"I can honestly say no," he said. "This is the place to be."

Welcome to Tempe, where the days are hot, the nights are cold, and the football game is the center of the college football universe.

That's another consequence of the BCS, isn't it? No other bowl seems to get any ink. No other bowl seems to matter.

The Rose Bowl is an afterthought. The Sugar Bowl is meaningless. The Orange Bowl had to invite Florida instead of Kansas State just to sell tickets.

But the Fiesta Bowl?

"It's huge," said Wilson, a former Melrose star. "You can feel it everywhere."

He's right, of course. You can feel it the moment you step off the plane.

It's not just the scalpers offering tickets for $1,000. It's not just the blimp doing practice laps in the sky. It's the media, the buzz around the town and the country.

• **DESERT DELIGHT:** Arizona's "Valley of the Sun" became home for a week to the nation's top media, the Vols and Seminoles and more than 70,000 of college football's greatest fans.

The Road to No. 1

Seven Days to Glory: December 28, 1998

The Road to No. 1

● **FRESH MANICURE:** Sun Devil Stadium was rolled, closely clipped and painted to host college football's first ever Division I-A National Championship Game.

ESPN is here. So is *Sports Illustrated*. There are four hotels given over to reporters. Heck, *ESPN* magazine ran a story about the sorts of things the Vols haul with them to the bowl games.

(Partial answer: 450 game and practice tapes, four video cameras, blocking dummies, blocking sleds, a dozen extra helmets, five cases of extra face masks, a dozen extra shoulder pads, three trunks filled with assorted types of cleats, and Future floor wax for polishing their helmets).

This is what comes with success, of course. This is what comes with a perfect season.

Everyone wants to talk about the Tennessee players. Everybody wants to hear the stories.

So the guy from the Boston paper is talking to Travis Henry about his trip from the bench to the starting backfield.

And the guy from the Chicago paper is asking Tee Martin about what it felt like to replace Peyton Manning.

And the guy from the Atlanta paper is asking Phil Fulmer if Tennessee has finally arrived as a national power.

"We hope we have," says the coach. "We like to think we've taken steps in that direction."

The good news for Tennessee fans is that the players seem to be handling it well, seem to be thriving in the spotlight.

Wilson couldn't stop smiling Tuesday. Peerless Price yucked it up with teammates. Jeff Hall told someone – with a straight face, mind you – that the key to the Vols' wins was "a seance ... We summon the great spirits."

Heck, even the coach seemed loose and happy. When someone asked about the SEC championship ring he wears on his right hand, Fulmer said he would like to replace it.

"We haven't even done the design for this year's SEC ring yet," he said. "We're hoping for the big one on there."

Time will tell if this mood lasts all week, of course. The Vols said they were relaxed before last year's Orange Bowl, too. Then they went out and got hammered by Nebraska.

But for now, they are soaking it in, enjoying their spot in the only bowl that really matters.

"I think we're the best team in the country," Wilson said. "I can't wait to have a chance to prove it."

113

Seven Days to Glory: December 29, 1998

Vols Enjoying Festive Atmosphere

By David Williams
The Commercial Appeal

TEMPE, Ariz., Dec. 29, 1998 – The big game is almost a week away. Heck, the big game is next year, if you want to be exact.

So maybe time will take the feel-good message from Al Wilson's mouth, or wipe the smile from Cedrick Wilson's face. But as of Tuesday afternoon -- six days and several hours from the No. 1 University of Tennessee football team's Fiesta Bowl clash with No. 2 Florida State – the Vols seemed calm as can be.

"Nobody should feel any pressure, for either team," said Al Wilson, middle linebacker and normally the team's most intense player. "We're all just college students. We're supposed to enjoy this. You know what I'm saying?

"I'm not going out there thinking it's the end of the world if we don't win the football game. I'm going out to have fun. It's my last collegiate game and I'm going out to enjoy."

Whether those prove to be words to play by, we'll have to check back on Jan. 4, when the Vols (12-0) meet the Seminoles (11-1) in Sun Devil Stadium for the national championship.

Maybe by then, Wilson will be growling – and the Vols, to a man, will be dealing in their own ways with the pressure of the biggest game of the season, the biggest game of their careers, the biggest in school history in a half-century or so.

Maybe by the evening of Jan. 4, Cedrick Wilson will concede that a 40-10 laugher might not be such a bad way to win it all.

As of today, Wilson, a sophomore wide receiver and former Melrose High star, wanted the drama high and the pressure packed.

"We're not looking for a blowout," he said. "I want it to be close. I want to win at the last second. I want it to be tight all the way down the stretch."

Asked if he also craves a starring role in that last-second victory, he shrugged.

"I don't care who it is, as long as we score. It could be Jeff Hall kicking a field goal."

Ah, Jeff Hall. The placekicker. The player most likely to be asked to pull Vol victory from his shoelaces while the world watches. Surely he's feeling more heat than what naturally occurs here in the Valley.

No, actually he sounds like he'd love it – game on the line, here's the snap, here's the kick, it's up and ...

Hall said he thinks about such situations no matter

> *I want to win at the last second. I want it to be tight all the way down the stretch.*
>
> **CEDRICK WILSON**

●**DEADLY AIM:** Tennessee's sure-footed kicker Jeff Hall may be called on to deliver a win for the Vols.

Seven Days to Glory: December 29, 1998

The Road to No. 1

the opposition, no matter the stakes. He said he thought about such things before the Vols played UAB.

Honestly now, there's no more pressure, this time around?

"Well, I'm sure there's going to be some more pressure and some more thought processes that go into the game," he said. "(But) I'm the type of guy who likes to play high-strung and real intense and everything.

"I think I'm a closet linebacker. That's how I like to play."

For now, though, they seem loose, these Vols. They sound at ease. They look relaxed in this starring role of No. 1 team in the nation.

Maybe it's the setting – the sun and the mountains and the heavenly weather. Maybe it's the timing – Florida State's best-in-the-nation defense is approaching, but is still several days from invasion.

Then again, maybe this is the most natural reaction in the world for a team that has faced pressure and skirted danger much of the season. The Vols won their season-opener over Syracuse in a comeback capped by a Hall field goal. They then beat Florida in overtime, again on a Hall field goal.

They had to rally to beat Arkansas, scramble to beat Mississippi State in the Southeastern Conference championship game. If pressure has any effect on this team, it must be all positive.

Is it any wonder Cedrick Wilson wants one more dramatic finish?

Is it any wonder Al Wilson looks to his last college game, the biggest game of his career, and wants, more than anything, to have fun.

"I feel like if you go out and have fun," he explained, "you play your best."

So there you have it, less than a week from kickoff: The Vols' emotional state, like the weather, is sunny with blue skies, and no storm clouds in sight. The Vols will tell you the long-range forecast calls for more of the same.

● **LAST-MINUTE THRILL: Cedrick Wilson, much like Peerless Price, is noted for making long TD catches.**

Seven Days to Glory: December 30, 1998

The Road to No. 1

Vol Corners Respect, But Don't Fear Warrick

By David Williams
The Commercial Appeal

TEMPE, Ariz., Dec. 30, 1998 – It's been said he's impossible to cover, a touchdown waiting to happen.

You don't need to tell University of Tennessee cornerback Steve Johnson about Florida State all-America receiver Peter Warrick. Johnson's heard the reviews and he's seen the film.

Two thumbs up? Or both hands, in helpless surrender?

"As a cornerback, you've got chills all through your body," Johnson said of facing Warrick when the No. 1 Vols (12-0) play the No. 2 Seminoles (11-1) for college football's national championship in Monday's Fiesta Bowl.

"It's a big challenge for me, and for Dwayne (Goodrich, UT cornerback) as well. We've been watching film all week on him. I think it's a challenge ... but as long as we go out there with a lot of confidence, I think we'll be all right."

When you get past the words of praise – when the chills subside – that's what you have: a Tennessee defense that's confident, wisely or not, that it can keep Warrick from running away with the biggest game of the season.

"We're going to be Tennessee," said John Chavis, the UT defensive coordinator. "And if you've seen us play, we're going to play a bunch of man-to-man, and that's going to be us. We're not going to change our philosophy going into this game.

"Certainly I think he may be the very best receiver in college football. We've played against good receivers all

● **TOO QUICK:** Peter Warrick, the Seminoles' brilliant receiver, was one of college football's most dangerous ballplayers when he had the ball.

Seven Days to Glory: December 30, 1998

year, and we're not going to change."

Will the Vols foil Warrick? Or simply become his foil?

It's one of the game's key matchups. Consider that Warrick caught 61 passes this season, averaging 20.2 yards per catch and 102.7 per game. He's a big-play receiver, a receiver who turns little plays into big ones.

"Peter Warrick is one of a kind," said Florida State quarterback Marcus Outzen. "You think you have him covered, but it's impossible to be as quick as he is, so he gets open."

Above all, he's a big-game receiver. Against the eight FSU opponents who spent time in the AP Top 25 this season, Warrick, a 6-0, 190-pound junior from Bradenton, Fla., averaged six catches for 123.4 yards, scoring 10 touchdowns.

In the biggest victory of the year – 23-12 over Florida on Nov. 21 – he even threw a fourth-quarter, 46-yard touchdown pass to Ron Dugans on a reverse. The pass didn't come out of nowhere – Warrick is a former prep quarterback.

Al Wilson, UT's all-America middle linebacker, was asked which FSU passer worries the Vols more, Outzen or Warrick.

"That's a good question," Wilson said.

●DIFFICULT ASSIGNMENT: Cornerback Steven Johnson is one of the Vol defenders whose assignment will be to keep Peter Warrick under wraps.

The Road to No. 1

But for all the respect, the Vols remain sure of their own defense. After all, they rank 17th nationally in pass efficiency defense, despite facing such vaunted air attacks as Kentucky and Florida.

Plus, the Vols' pass rush has been rather adept at hurrying and harrying quarterbacks, meaning Outzen and Warrick may have to work quickly.

"We are a pressure defense," Chavis said. "The pressure's got to be a factor. We can't give the quarterback all day to throw the football. Because if we do, they're going to complete it.

"If you give them enough time to throw and they complete it, the receivers are good enough that they're going to make a run. So it's all tied together with our front seven, and the pressure we've got to generate. That's a big part of our coverage package also."

Does that sound like a reasonable plan for containing Warrick? Well, it makes sense to the man himself.

"You can't put all of the focus on trying to stop me," Warrick said, "because we have other great receivers in (tailback) Travis Minor and Laveranues Coles. If I have to make big plays, that's what I'll do. If I have to block for Travis Minor, I'll do that, too.

"Whatever it takes to win."

Seven Days to Glory: December 31, 1998

Memphis Has Own Fiesta MVP

By Geoff Calkins
The Commercial Appeal

TEMPE, Ariz., Dec. 31, 1998 – Cedrick Wilson for mayor.

You think I am kidding?

I am not kidding.

I am thinking about slogans. I am dreaming up bumper stickers. I am wondering if he would let me manage the campaign.

The idea came to me a while ago. But today, well, this morning cinched it.

Wilson was sitting in Sun Devil Stadium, basking in the sweet Arizona sun.

Someone asked Wilson if he'd ever been to Arizona before.

"Oh, no," he said.

Then someone asked Wilson if he thought it was pretty.

"Oh, yes," he said.

Then Wilson stopped the person before he could say another word.

"It's pretty," he said. "But I wouldn't trade it for Memphis."

That's what he said! Unprompted! A person from Memphis, on a national stage, saying nice things about his city!

So, as I said, Wilson for mayor.

"That would be OK," said Wilson. "I love Memphis. I really do."

Wilson grew up in Orange Mound, led Melrose High to its very first state football title, then turned himself into a star receiver at Tennessee.

Tee Martin looks to him in clutch situations. The coaches show film of Wilson blocking to the offensive line. Vanderbilt coach Woody Widenhofer said Wilson could become the best Tennessee receiver of the decade.

But on the verge of playing for a national title, Wilson will tell you he never has enjoyed the game of football as much as he did when he played high school ball in Memphis.

"It was great," he says. "I love that community. I'll never feel anything like that again."

This is how he talks. This is what makes him so special. He grew up in a dicey part of town. He remembers hearing gun shots ringing through the night. But ask him if it was tough to grow up in Orange Mound, and he looks at you as if you are nuts.

● **THE BEST:** Tennessee's Peerless Price (37) celebrates with teammate Jeremaine Copeland (6) after scoring a touchdown during the second half of the Volunteers' 22-3 victory over Georgia in Athens, Ga.

31 Thursday December 1998

DAY 4

7:00 a.m.	Football Staff Meeting
7:30	Wake-Up Call – Players
8:00	General Staff Meeting
8:00-9:30	Meetings
9:30-10:00	Brunch – MANDATORY – Grand Ballroom C & D YOU WILL NOT HAVE AN OPPORTUNITY TO EAT AGAIN UNTIL AFTER PRACTICE
10:00	Buses Depart For Media Day @ Sun Devil Stadium Dress: Game Jerseys & Black JMN Pants
10:30-11:30	Media Day @ Sun Devil Stadium
11:45	Buses Depart for Practice Turn in Game Jersey @ Practice Site
12:15 p.m.	Begin Dressing & Taping
12:45	Flex Practice Media Interviews After Practice (If Necessary) Weights to Follow (Offense – Two Deep)
3:45	Buses Depart for Hotel
4:00	Meal @ Hotel – MANDATORY – Grand Ballroom C & D
6:00	Shuttle Service to New Year's Block Party Begins Shuttles will depart & Pick Up On a Continuous Cycle beginning @ 8:30 p.m.
8:30	Snack – Team Hospitality Room
11:00	Player Hospitality Room Closes
12:30 a.m.	Last Shuttles Depart from Block Party PLAYERS MUST BE ON THE 12:30 SHUTTLE
1:00	Bed Check (Captains)

Bowl games:
11:30 a.m.	Liberty Bowl (Brigham Young vs Tulane, ESPN)
12:00 n	Sun Bowl (Southern Cal vs TCU, CBS)
3:00 p.m.	Peach Bowl (Virginia vs Georgia, ESPN)
6:30 p.m.	Independence Bowl (Ole Miss vs Texas Tech, ESPN)

BEAT THE SEMINOLES!

Seven Days to Glory: December 31, 1998

> "
> *I'm not that into politics. I think I'd better stick to football.*
>
> CEDRICK WILSON
> "

"Awwww, no," he says. "I love Orange Mound. There's no place like it in the world."

It's surprising, isn't it? Surprising and refreshing, too?

So many Memphians tear their city down. So many Memphians who have so much. But here's a guy who grew up with comparatively little – who says his mother worked a series of just-get-by jobs to keep her five kids in food and clothes – and he thinks of Memphis as a sort of Xanadu on the Mississippi.

"I can't wait to go back," he says. "I go every chance I get."

Back at the stadium, the Wilson-for-mayor campaign is off to a slow start.

It's not that his teammates don't like him, mind you. It's just that their endorsements seem, well, a little off.

Spencer Riley says Wilson is a vicious blocker. But is a vicious blocker what the city needs?

Fellow Melrose graduate Kevin Taylor says Wilson can catch anything thrown his way.

But does a mayor catch anything but flak?

Even Wilson says he's developing some misgivings.

"I'm not that into politics," he says. "I think I'd better stick to football."

So we'll put it aside now, let the campaign wait until the time is right.

But if Wilson catches the winning touchdown Monday night, if the cameras seek him out, if he tells the Disney folks that now that he's won the Fiesta Bowl, he's off to Memphis, Tenn.?

Well, just remember. Wilson for mayor.

You heard it here first.

The Road to No. 1

Fulmer To Receive $6 Million Contract

By David Williams and Geoff Calkins
The Commercial Appeal

TEMPE, Arix., Dec. 31, 1998 – Tennessee coach Phillip Fulmer, whose No. 1-ranked Volunteers play Florida State for the national championship Monday night in the Fiesta Bowl, signed a new six-year contract today worth more than $1 million a year.

Fulmer and athletics director Doug Dickey worked out the contract in Arizona during the team's preparations for the Fiesta Bowl.

The contact will raise Fulmer's total pay by about $200,000 and make him the second-highest paid coach in the Southeastern Conference. Florida's Steve Spurrier makes nearly $2 million a year.

Fulmer's new base salary will be $175,000; radio and television commitments pay $400,000; apparel and shoe contracts pay $250,000; and he gets a $250,000 annual retention bonus that began after the 1997 season.

That adds up to $1,075,000. Other benefits, such as a free car and complimentary tickets, bring the total value to more than $1.1 million, according to the university.

Fulmer is finishing his sixth full season as the Tennessee head coach. He has an overall record of 66-11, and the best winning percentage of any active Division 1-A coach.

"The contract is in keeping with the economic standards of college coaching and is deserved," Dickey said.

"No institution is more proud of its coach than we at the University of Tennessee are about Phillip Fulmer for the way he has recruited, coached and managed the program."

• **TOP DOLLAR:** UT coach Phil Fulmer's new $6 million contract made him the second-highest paid coach in the SEC.

Seven Days to Glory: January 1, 1999

Vols Look Back for Motivation

By David Williams
The Commercial Appeal

TEMPE, Ariz., Jan. 1, 1999 – Embarrassed. Humiliated and harassed.

Beaten up, knocked down, shoved around.

Where would the University of Tennessee be if it hadn't gone through all that in last year's Orange Bowl, a 42-17 blowout by a Nebraska team that shared the national championship?

Maybe not here, in Monday's Fiesta Bowl, playing Florida State for this season's crown.

"We had some great players," said offensive guard Mercedes Hamilton, "and they spanked us. ... It was an eye-opener."

Wide receiver Peerless Price said, "They embarrassed us on national TV. We had to have a sense of urgency. If not, we wouldn't be here today. We had to have a sense of urgency to go in the weight room, get better, get stronger, get more physical."

It may seem an odd source of strength and inspiration – a 25-point loss from which a nation tuned out before the fourth quarter, some from boredom, others for more humanitarian reasons.

But it's a source of strength, the top-ranked Vols say, because it's made them stronger. It exposed them to the highest level of college football and taught them lessons you just don't get at the Citrus Bowl.

"We didn't know how the big dogs play," Price said.

One popular notion here is that second-ranked Florida State has a big edge in big-game experience, and the Seminoles certainly have plenty of it. They won the 1993 national championship and played for the 1996 title. They've finished in the top four of the AP poll for 11 straight years.

Tennessee is trying to win its first consensus national title since 1951, and last year's Orange Bowl was the championship game from the Nebraska perspective.

This is not a notion that Florida State embraces, however.

"They know how it feels to lose in the national championship game," said Seminole cornerback Mario Edwards. "You're even that much more hungry the next time."

FSU split end Ron Dugans said, "I know that motivates them, because they went to a big game and did-

● **A LESSON LEARNED: The Vols' 42-17 runaway loss to Nebraska in the 1998 Orange Bowl prepared them for the steely tests of the journey to the 1999 Fiesta Bowl.**

The Road to No. 1

Seven Days to Glory: January 1, 1999

n't win. They came out this year and went 12-0, so that motivated them."

That 12-0 record was built on big games – a season-opening victory at Syracuse, an overtime win that ended a five-year losing streak to Florida, a rally against Arkansas.

It was built, too, with first-year starting QB Tee Martin replacing No. 1 NFL draft pick Peyton Manning, and with star Jamal Lewis suffering a season-ending knee injury in the fourth game.

And so the Vols completed the school's first unbeaten regular season since 1956, and finished atop both national polls.

"I don't know if I could say we wouldn't be here if it wasn't for the Orange Bowl," said middle linebacker Al Wilson, "but it had a big part to it. The Orange Bowl was a learning experience.

"It told us that we had to go out and prepare ourselves a little harder in the offseason to be one of the elite college teams. And that's what we did this offseason. We went out and worked as hard as we possibly could, and kept our focus. Every player was determined to be the best player they possibly could.

"That Nebraska game really put us over the hump."

Having spent a night on the highest national stage, the Vols seemed determined to get back and try again.

The season itself is proof that it worked – Tennessee has a perfect record, something coach Bobby Bowden's Seminoles, for all their glory, haven't achieved. But the Vols know they need to win this game to join the elite – and they plan to do just that.

These Vols aren't wide-eyed. They're not just happy to be here. The hype of a huge game doesn't faze them, because they played in last year's Orange Bowl. They don't seem to wonder whether they belong on the field with Florida State, because the Orange Bowl taught them what to expect at this level.

"To get the respect I think we deserve," said UT cornerback Steve Johnson, "we're going to have to go out there and beat a team like Florida State. I think one of the main reasons we're the underdog is because coach Bowden and those guys are in the championship mix every year."

There are more tangible reasons Florida State is favored, of course. The Seminoles have the nation's No. 1 defense, allowing only 214.8 yards per game. The offense features All-American flanker Peter Warrick.

The Vols can make a strong case, though, that the main difference between these two teams is recent history and reputation – FSU's constant presence in the national title chase.

Consider: Tennessee's defense ranked 17th in the nation, as is its rushing attack. It's a team with balance, quickness and close-game cool. And the Vols know what to expect from their quarterback, while Florida State may have some doubts about Marcus Outzen, making his third start since Chris Weinke was injured in November.

Yes, the Seminoles have more experience at this sort of game. But the Vols will tell you they got quite a jolt of it last Jan. 2, and it made them stronger, better, more determined.

And, they'll tell you, history may even be on their side. Florida, remember, was blown out by Nebraska, 62-24, in the 1995 national championship game. The next season, the Gators won it all – beating Florida State, 52-20.

"It's the same scenario," Price said. "Hopefully we can do that."

> "That Nebraska game really put us over the hump.
>
> — AL WILSON

● **VICTORY LAP:** Linebacker Al Wilson carried the Vols' flag around Vanderbilt Stadium after Tennessee routed the Commodores, 41-0, to complete an 11-0 season.

Seven Days to Glory: January 2, 1999

Price Out to Win Receiver Battle

By David Williams
The Commercial Appeal

TEMPE, Ariz., Jan. 2, 1999 – University of Tennessee wide receiver Peerless Price is looking to steal some thunder.

He also might want to see about getting his name back.

Ask around, and surely you'll be told that Florida State all-American Peter Warrick is the real peerless receiver in Monday's Fiesta Bowl.

"He's real good," said Price, the top-ranked Volunteers' leading receiver, said of Warrick. "He runs great routes, he catches the ball well, and his biggest asset is, he makes something happen after the catch.

"I hope our guys can contain him. If not, it's going to be a long night for us."

But if this national championship football game is Warrick's stage, it may be Price's opportunity to show the nation that he's also quite the catch.

"I know I can do some of the things he does," Price said. "But he's a high-profile player on that team and we're a team of no stars. He can do some things better than me, I can do some things better than him."

What can Price do better?

He shook his head and said, "I ain't going to get into that."

So he'd rather show than tell, but it won't be easy.

Warrick, a 6-0, 190-pound junior from Bradenton, Fla., caught 61 passes this season for 1,232 yards – a 20.2 per-catch average – with 12 touchdowns. FSU coach Bobby Bowden said he might be the nation's most dangerous receiver, and the most difficult to tackle.

Warrick on Warrick: "When you have God's gift, you have to use it to the best of your ability. Every time I get the ball, I feel like I have to do something with it."

Whenever Warrick is interviewed in the days leading up to the Fiesta Bowl, the topics include his great talent and his decision whether to skip his senior season for the NFL.

Whenever Price is interviewed, a topic invariably is what he thinks of Warrick. By the end of the week, the question seemed to be getting stale to Price, a 6-0, 183-pounder from Dayton, Ohio.

Asked once too often about Warrick, Price said, "I don't watch him on film."

●**SEC CHAMPS:** Vol receivers Peerless Price (37) and Cedrick Wilson (14) trade "high fives" after Price's game-winning 41-yard TD reception against Mississippi State.

2 — Saturday January 1999 — DAY 6

7:00 a.m.	Football Staff Meeting
8:00	General Staff Meeting
7:30-9:00	Breakfast – MANDATORY – GRAND BALLROOM C & D Dress: Black JMN Pants & Black Patagonia Fleece Top
8:30	Six Players Depart for Press Conference @ Tempe Mission Palms (Goodrich, A. Wilson, T. Martin, Hall, Bryson, C. Wilson)
9:00-10:00	Press Conference @ Tempe Mission Palms
10:00	Six Players Depart Press Conference for Hotel
10:30-11:45	Meetings
11:45	Lunch — MANDATORY — GRAND BALLROOM C & D
1:00 p.m.	Buses Depart for Practice
1:15	Begin Dressing & Taping Interviews (Coaches Only — No Player Interviews)
1:45	Flex Practice
4:45	Buses Depart for Hotel Dress: Casual
5:00	Fiesta Bowl Steak Fry & Cookout – MANDATORY – GRAND BALLROOM C & D
6:00	Player Hospitality Room Opens
7:00	Buses Depart for Local Theater or Watch Orange Bowl Movies @ Local Theater
8:30	MANDATORY SNACK FOLLOWING ORANGE BOWL GAME — Hospitality Room
10:30	Player Hospitality Room Closes
11:00	Bed Check

Other events:

9:00 a.m.	Buses Depart for Fiesta Bowl Parade
11:00	Microage Fiesta Bowl Parade @ Central Avenue

Bowl games:

6:00	Orange Bowl (Florida vs. Syracuse, ABC)

BEAT THE SEMINOLES!

Seven Days to Glory: January 2, 1999

Asked once more whether this was a game to show the nation his own skills, Price said, "Yeah, you always take that into consideration when you're going against one of the best receivers in the country.

"But that isn't my focus in the ballgame. My focus in the ballgame is making some plays for my team to win, and that's what I'm going out there to do."

Price has made those plays all season, including a 41-yard, fourth-quarter catch against Mississippi State that sent the Vols to a victory in the SEC Championship Game. He had six catches for 97 yards.

For the season, he had 61 catches – the same as Warrick – although his yardage was lower, at 920 overall and 15.1 per catch. While Warrick was an all-American, Price was second-team all-SEC.

But if there's a big talent gap here, Price's teammates don't see it.

"Every national championship team I've watched when I was a kid growing up, and even as a player, they've got a big-play guy. For us, Peerless is that person," said UT quarterback Tee Martin.

"To me, when he's covered, he's not covered. We have a relationship where I know where to put the ball, and he kind of knows where to expect it to drop."

Which is something Price does better than Warrick, said UT receiver Cedrick Wilson.

"Warrick, once he gets the ball in his hands, he's dangerous," Wilson said. "But I don't think he's a very good deep ball go-getter. ... Peerless can go and get it."

The game itself, of course, decides the national championship. But this game-within-the-game is shaping up nicely, too. Who can make the biggest and best catches? Who can make the game-breaking play?

Warrick or Price?

Monday night, we see whether they're peers, or whether one is peerless.

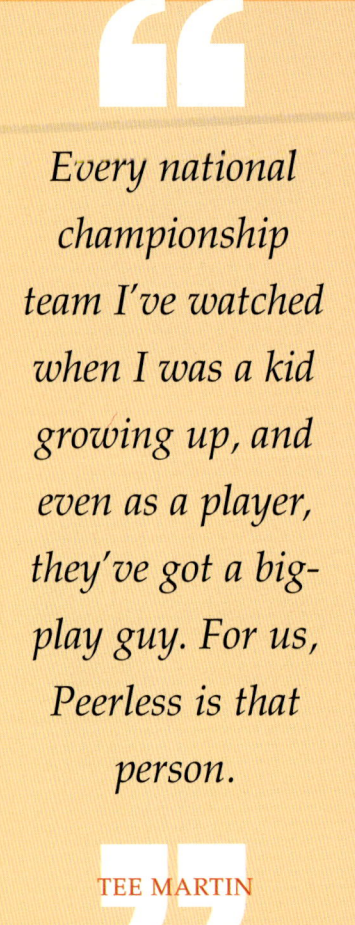

> *Every national championship team I've watched when I was a kid growing up, and even as a player, they've got a big-play guy. For us, Peerless is that person.*
>
> — TEE MARTIN

● **PLAYMAKERS:** Receivers coach Pat Washington instructs Jeremaine Copeland (6), Peerless Price (37) and Eric Parker (80) at practice prior to the Fiesta Bowl.

Seven Days to Glory: January 3, 1999

Us vs. Them? Take Us

By Geoff Calkins
The Commercial Appeal

TEMPE, Ariz., Jan. 3, 1999 -- Tennessee is better.

I am not just talking about quarterbacks. I am not just talking about offensive linemen. I am not just talking about tonight's college football championship game.

No, I'm talking about all the rest: The arts, the food, the celebrities.

Take newspaper writers, for instance. Start with that.

Tennessee had Grantland Rice. Florida has Dave Barry.

Imagine if Barry had covered that legendary football game between Notre Dame and Army in 1924.

"Outlined against a blue-gray October sky, the Four Horsemen rode again. In dramatic lore, they were known as Famine, Pestilence, Destruction and Death. These are only aliases. Their real names are Booger. And I am not making this up."

See what I mean?

Tennessee is better.

Not just in football. In everything.

And we are not making this up.

Jimmy Buffet, above, Elvis, right.

SINGERS
US: Elvis Presley
THEM: Jimmy Buffett
Presley sang *Love me tender*. Buffett sang *Why don't we get drunk and ...*
EDGE: Tennessee

FAMOUS CROCKETTS
US: Davy
THEM: Sonny
Davy Crockett worked alongside Sam Houston and Jim Bowie. Sonny Crockett worked alongside Ricardo Tubbs.
EDGE: Tennessee

STATEHOOD
US: 1796
THEM: 1845
During the War of 1812, the British used Florida as a base of operations. So Tennessee's Andrew Jackson captured Pensacola, leading to Florida's secession to the United States.
EDGE: Tennessee

LIQUID REFRESHMENT
US: Jack Daniel's
THEM: Orange Juice
A day without Jack Daniel's is like a day without, um, moonshine?
EDGE: Tennessee

PRESIDENTS
US: Andrew Johnson, Andrew Jackson and James K. Polk
THEM: Still waiting
Thomas Dewey did die in Florida, if that counts for anything.
EDGE: Tennessee

TRIALS
US: The Scopes trial.
THEM: The William Kennedy Smith trial
If they had the Scopes trial today, you can be sure we'd have Greta Van Susteren down here, but quick.
EDGE: Tennessee

BASEBALL TEAMS
US: The Redbirds
THEM: The Marlins
The Redbirds have a bigger payroll.
EDGE: Tennessee

The Road to No. 1

3 — DAY 7 — Sunday January 1999

8:00 a.m.	General Staff Meeting
8:30-9:00	Fulmer Press Conference
8:30-9:30	ABC/ESPN Game Crew Interviews @ Hotel (Fulmer, Chavis & Sanders)
8:00-9:30	Breakfast – MANDATORY – GRAND BALLROOM C & D Dress: Coat & Tie
9:30	Buses Depart for Local Church
10:00	Arrive: North Phoenix Baptist Church
10:30	Church Service @ North Phoenix Baptist Church (Rev. Dan Yeary – Pastor))
11:30	Buses Depart Church for Hotel
12:00-1:00	Lunch – MANDATORY – GRAND BALLROOM C & D Dress: Black JMN Pants & Grey SEC Championship Sweat Top
2:15 p.m.	Fulmer & Team Depart for NCAA YES Clinic
2:45	Fulmer & Team Arrive at NCAA YES Clinic Fulmer to Make Brief Speech Players to Sign Autographs
3:00-4:00	NCAA Pre-game Meeting – Stadium Press Box
3:15	Fulmer & Team Depart for Walk-Thru
3:30	Dress for Walk-Thru – Sun Devil Stadium
4:00-5:00	Walk-Thru @ Sun Devil Stadium
6:15	Dinner – MANDATORY – GRAND BALLROOM C & D
7:30	Meetings
8:30	Snack – GRAND BALLROOM C & D
12:00	Bed Check – In Bed – Lights Out!

Other events:

8:00 a.m.	Group Departs Hotel for Grand Canyon Tour
11:00	Group Departs for VIP Golf Outing
4:00 p.m	Group Returns to Hotel from Grand Canyon Tour
6:00	Official Party Dinner @ Hotel – Terraza Patio Tent

BEAT THE SEMINOLES!

Seven Days to Glory: January 3, 1999

AMUSEMENT PARKS
US: Libertyland
THEM: Disney World
Two words: Zippin Pippin
EDGE: Tennessee

DESIGNING WOMEN
US: Dixie Carter
THEM: Delta Burke
Dixie's cuter.
EDGE: Tennessee

GOLF TOURNAMENTS
US: The FedEx St. Jude
THEM: The Doral Open
Just try to buy a Pronto Pup at the Doral Open.
EDGE: Tennessee

MOVIES
US: The Firm
THEM: Ace Ventura
Wasn't Ace Ventura the movie in which Jim Carrey talked out of his butt?
EDGE: Tennessee

MOUNTAINS
US: The Smokies
THEM: Space Mountain
You don't have to wait in line at the Smokies.
EDGE: Tennessee

PRESIDENTIAL APOLOGISTS
US: Al Gore
THEM: Janet Reno
At least it's part of Gore's job description.
EDGE: Tennessee

Attorney General Janet Reno, above, and Vice President Al Gore.

The Road to No. 1

MUSIC
US: Patsy Cline, Aretha Franklin, Bill Monroe, Minnie Pearl, Gregg Allman, Dolly Parton, Hank Williams, Tina Turner, W. C. Handy, Loretta Lynn, Bessie Smith
THEM: Jim Stafford
They say Stafford had a pretty big hit with I don't like Spiders and Snakes.
EDGE: Tennessee

BASKETBALL STARS
US: Penny Hardaway
THEM: Penny Hardaway
Our Penny was never locked out.
EDGE: Tennessee

SOLDIERS
US: Sergeant York
THEM: William Calley
This is getting to be a rout, isn't it?
EDGE: Tennessee

GULF COAST
US: Mud Island
THEM: Destin
In Destin, you can swim at the edge of the Gulf of Mexico. In Mud Island, you can do a belly flop right in the middle.
EDGE: Tennessee

TOURIST ATTRACTIONS
US: Graceland
THEM: Gatorland
At Gatorland, outside Kissimmee, Fla., they hang a chicken carcass on a clothesline to coax 15-foot alligators to leap out of the water. They call this the Gator Jumparoo.
EDGE: Tennessee

CUISINE
US: Barbecue
THEM: Stone Crabs
That settles it. A plate of barbecue at Corky's will cost you $6.99. A plate of three large stone crabs at Joe's will cost you $30.95. And the sweet potato is $7 extra.
EDGE: Tennessee

Jim Stafford, above, and Hank Wiliams.

Fiesta Bowl
National C

hampions

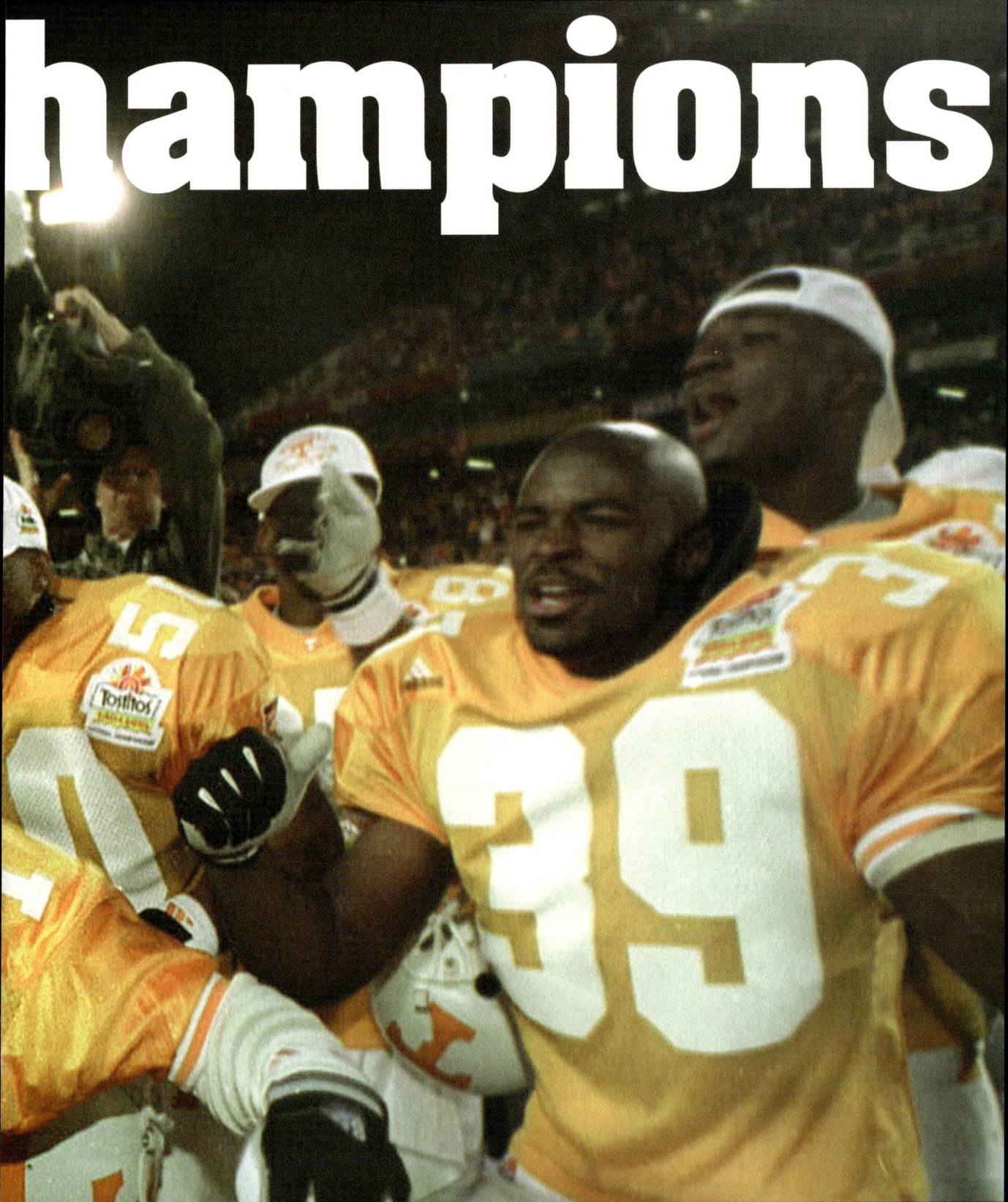

Champions:
The 47-Year Wait Is Over

The Road to No. 1

FIESTA BOWL
NATIONAL CHAMPIONSHIP

TENNESSEE	**23**
FLORIDA STATE	**16**

By Mike Strange
The Knoxville News-Sentinel

TEMPE, Ariz., Jan. 4, 1999 – The doubters are silenced, finally. Tennessee came to the desert certain there would be a national championship for the taking.

They were right. It was no mirage.

A few minutes after midnight back in Knoxville – four months to the day they began their unlikely quest with an unlikely win at Syracuse – the No. 1-ranked Vols completed their perfect season of destiny.

A 23-16 win over favored Florida State in the Fiesta Bowl was the crowning accomplishment – literally.

The victory clinched an automatic No. 1 ranking in the final coaches poll as champions of the Bowl Championship Series title game.

The Associated Press media poll will make the 13-0 Vols unanimous national champions today.

The school's first title since 1951 was achieved before an orange-tinted majority in the Fiesta Bowl record crowd of 80,470 at Sun Devil Stadium.

The Vols punched up 392 yards of offense against the nation's No. 1-ranked defense – which had allowed an average of 214 – and got timely big plays from its defense.

• **HEARTBREAKER: Peerless Price's 4 receptions for 199 yards and 2 TD's sealed the Vols' win over FSU.**

The Fiesta Bowl

Tee Martin threw touchdown passes to Peerless Price and Shawn Bryson, and Dwayne Goodrich got another with an interception return.

The Vols held FSU (11-2) to 253 yards, frustrated redshirt freshman quarterback Marcus Outzen and, best of all, held All-American receiver Peter Warrick to one solitary first-half catch for 7 yards.

"I want to say an unbelievable thank you to the crowd of loyal Tennessee Volunteers," said coach Phillip Fulmer, clutching the championship trophy.

"It's 47 years since Tennessee football has brought one of these home. We've got a special place for it."

Tennessee nursed a 14-9 lead into the fourth quarter, then closed the deal with sudden authority.

Martin hooked up with Price on a Fiesta Bowl-record 79-yard touchdown with 9:17 remaining.

Tennessee's edge was 20-9 after the extra-point attempt was blocked, but the Vols would get more from Jeff Hall soon enough.

● **SETBACK: Dwayne Goodrich was forced to leave the game after a leg injury in the second quarter.**

On FSU's first snap after the kickoff, Shaun Ellis stripped Outzen and Billy Ratliff recovered at the Seminoles' 28.

Travis Stephens, who rushed for 60 yards, found a rare hole and scampered 18 yards to the 8, but there would be no more room to move.

Hall drilled a 23-yard field goal and a 23-9 looked awfully strong with 6:01 to play.

Florida State, nevertheless, would make things interesting.

Aided by a personal foul against UT on the kickoff return, the Seminoles took over at midfield and hit the big play on a third-down pass to Ron Dugans that covered 39 yards to the Tennessee 7.

Outzen got the touchdown from there on a draw play. After the PAT, it was 23-16 with 3:42 left.

● **CAN'T STOP HIM: John Finlayson (96) rumbles for 14 yards and a key first down against the Seminoles.**

The Road to No. 1

The Seminoles then almost shocked the Vols with a successful onsides kick. Tennessee was awarded possession because Florida State touched the ball before it advanced 10 yards.

At the FSU 33, the Vols pulled their own mild surprise, flipping a 22-yard pass to Bryson on fourth-and-1.

Travis Henry fumbled the ball to Florida State with 1:29 left, but Steve Johnson went and got it back on the next play, intercepting an Outzen deep ball.

That left 76 seconds to occupy and the Vols were only happy to do so.

"This team has consistently found ways to win," said Fulmer.

"It's not one or two guys. It's a whole football team

The Fiesta Bowl

● **TIGHT COVERAGE:** Dwayne Goodrich and the Vol defense held Peter Warrick to 1 reception and 7 yards.

believing they can get it done and working hard to get it done."

The Vols and Seminoles spent the first quarter feeling out each other. Tennessee's first possession was prolonged when FSU safety Dexter Jackson was flagged for roughing punter David Leaverton.

Hall missed a 33-yard field goal attempt, but the Vols' first defensive series was impressive, including a 30-yard loss on one forlorn FSU play. The Seminoles punted, Tennessee took over at its 39 and crossed midfield again, aided by a Seminole personal foul.

Henry got a first down at the Florida State 32, but two plays later fumbled and the Seminoles pounced.

FSU's next two possessions were three-and-out and with 1:07 left in the first quarter, the Vols hit the big one.

Martin found Price running deep for a 76-yard gainer to the Florida State 12. The Seminoles held at the 7 and Hall kicked a 24-yard field goal on the second snap of the second quarter.

However, the Seminoles were again guilty of roughing the kicker. Tennessee took the points off the board in favor of a first-and-goal at the 4.

After an incompletion on first down, Martin rolled left and flipped a pass to fullback Bryson, who sprinted for the corner of the goal line and made it.

It took only 25 seconds for the Vols to double their lead.

Florida State's first play after the kickoff was a 29-yard Outzen completion. Its second was a disaster.

Outzen threw in the right flat for Warrick, but Goodrich stepped in front for the interception at his 46 and had 54 yards of clear sailing.

That made it 14-0 with 13:40 left in the half.

The Seminoles borrowed a page – make that two

pages – from Mississippi State in the SEC championship game to get back in the game.

The first was Derrick Gibson's interception of a Martin pass and 43-yard return to the UT 3. Fullback William McCray got the touchdown from the 1.

The conversion was botched, however. Florida State was penalized 5 yards for procedure, leaving Janikowski, the Lou Groza Award winner, with a 25-yard PAT. It appeared to be deflected by UT's Ellis and struck the crossbar. Tennessee's lead remained at 14-6 with 8:59 in the half.

The Vols' next drive was sabotaged by three procedure penalties. The third nullified a successful Leaverton punt.

Leaverton was forced to re-kick, and the ever-dangerous Warrick juked his way 51 yards to the UT 27 before Leaverton made a touchdown-saving tackle.

From there, FSU's drive was no thing of beauty. The Seminoles converted on fourth-and-inches at the 6, but were then guilty of two procedure penalties of their own.

Throw in a Corey Terry tackle of Outzen for a loss and Janikowski was left to kick a 34-yard field goal to make it 14-9. The scoring drive was one for the books: 10 yards in 10 plays.

The third quarter produced nothing resembling a scoring threat.

Tennessee couldn't take advantage of good field position.

Florida State couldn't penetrate a UT defense that had lost Goodrich (ankle) and reserve tackle Ron Greene (knee).

The fourth quarter began with momentum and field position swinging Tennessee's way, as Leaverton punted the ball dead inside the FSU 1.

The Seminoles punted it back and Eric Parker's 17-yard return put UT in business only 35 yards from the game-icing touchdown.

The Vols tried to get it all at once and got burned. Martin's pass into the end zone was juggled by Price and intercepted by Jackson, who brought it back to the 26.

Three plays later, the Seminoles were at the Tennessee 26. They wouldn't get any closer.

Darwin Walker roared in to sack Outzen for a 10-yard loss on third down, driving the Seminoles back out of Janikowski's field-goal range.

FSU punted and three plays later, Martin and Price connected for the big one.

The Road to No. 1

```
Florida State  0   9   0   7   —  16
Tennessee      0  14   0   9   —  23
```

FIRST QUARTER
No Scoring

SECOND QUARTER
Tenn-Bryson 4-yard pass from T. Martin (Hall kick), 14:05.
Tenn-Goodrich 54-yard interception return (Hall kick), 13:40.
FSU-McCray 1-yard run (Janikowski kick failed), 8:59.
FSU-Janikowski 34-yard field goal, 1:17.

THIRD QUARTER
No Scoring

FOURTH QUARTER
Tenn-Price 79 pass from T. Martin (kick failed), 9:17.
Tenn-Hall 23-yard field goal, 6:01.
FSU-Outzen 7-yard run (Janikowski kick), 3:42.

GAME STATS

	FSU	Tennessee
First Downs	13	16
Rushed-Yards	41-108	45-114
Passing Yardage	145	278
Comp-Att-Int	9-22-2	11-19-2
Return Yards	120	108
Punts-Avg.	9-39.8	5-38.0
Fumbles-Lost	4-1	3-2
Penalties-Yards	12-110	9-55
Time of Possession	28:50	31:10

INDIVIDUAL STATS

RUSHING: Florida State, Minor 15-83, P. Warrick 1-11, Mccray 4-9, Coles 2-4, Glenn 1-2, Outzen 18-minus 1. Tennessee, Stephens 13-60, Henry 19-28, T. Martin 10-19, Bryson 3-7.

PASSING: Florida State, Outzen 9-22-2-145. Tennessee, T. Martin 11-18-2-278, Henry 0-1-0-0.

RECEIVING: Florida State, Dugans 6-135, Mccray 1-11, P Warrick 1-7, Minor 1-minus 8. Tennessee, Price 4-199, Bryson 3-34, Copeland 1-15, Finlayson 1-14, Henry 1-9, C Wilson 1-7.

The Fiesta Bowl

The Road to No. 1

UT Has a New Fight Song: 'We're No. 1'

By John Adams
The Knoxville News-Sentinel

TEMPE, Ariz., Jan. 4, 1999 — You have seen it all before.

You have seen the thunderous defense and the lightning strikes from quarterback Tee Martin to wide receiver Peerless Price. You have seen the fourth-quarter stranglehold that squeezed victories from Syracuse, Florida, Arkansas and Mississippi State.

You saw it again tonight at Sun Devil Stadium in the Fiesta Bowl. The only difference was the bigger stage.

On the biggest stage in college football, Florida State's No. 1 ranked defense was upstaged by the defense of the nation's No. 1 team; UT Peerless Price surpassed FSU All-American wide receiver Peter Warrick; the Vols beat the Seminoles, 23-16; and *Rocky Top* reverberated throughout Sun Devil Stadium.

But for the first time in 47 years, the Vols could shout something sweeter than *Rocky Top*. They could chant, "We're No. 1."

UT deserved that No. 1 ranking after it beat Georgia, 22-3, way back in early October. By then, it already had victories over Florida and Syracuse as well.

Yet the Vols didn't become a complete team until that Saturday afternoon in Athens, Ga. Two questions were answered in passing that day.

Yes, Tee Martin could pass. Yes, UT's secondary could cover the pass.

Martin threw for two touchdowns, and the UT defense wrecked the Georgia offense and quarterback Quincy Carter, who had played sensationally the

● **LOOSE BALL: Raynoch Thompson (46) scrambles for Laveranues Coles' fumble.**

147

The Fiesta Bowl

week before against LSU.

The same virtues came to the fore against Florida State. Martin teamed up with Price on a 79-yard touchdown pass that gave the Vols a 20-9 lead with 9:17 to play in the game. Three quarters earlier, Martin and Price hooked up on a 76-yard pass that suddenly changed the field position in a game where two great defenses made field position vital.

Price had four catches for 199 yards. The much-heralded Warrick managed only one catch for 7 yards.

UT's secondary didn't just cover Warrick. It outscored him. Cornerback Dwayne Goodrich returned a second-quarter interception 54 yards for a touchdown.

It was typical defense for a national champion that was clutch, rather than dominant. But this schedule wasn't designed for dominance.

The Vols beat two top 10 teams, Florida and Florida State; beat three other Top 25 teams — Georgia, Arkansas and Syracuse; and three more bowl teams — Kentucky, Alabama and Mississippi State.

They won four games with fourth-quarter comebacks. They won with great team chemistry, luck, talent and a powerful mixture of fire and ice.

As fiery as this team could be on game day, it could be just as cool when composure was needed. Moreover, it evinced a corporate like coldness in preparation. "We're here to take care of business," one player after another repeated during their week in the desert.

In that respect, these Vols seemed less like their predecessor and more like the Nebraska team that drubbed UT in the 1998 Orange Bowl to win the national championship. Both champions did what was necessary. The Cornhuskers needed to win big; the Vols needed to win.

This victory puts UT on a different plateau — a very, small plateau. The Vols already had the other identifying characteristics of an elite program. They had a long trail bowl appearances, a slew of high picks in the NFL draft, and string of Top 25 finishes.

Now they have something else: a national championship.

● **SIDELINE TALK: An intense Vol coach Phillip Fulmer instructs John Finlayson (96) during the third quarter.**

The Road to No. 1

The Fiesta Bowl

Seminoles Crumbled on Offense

By Gary Lundy
The Knoxville News-Sentinel

TEMPE, Ariz., Jan. 4, 1999 — Florida State's offense was like the broken pieces of Tostitos that littered the field after tonight's Fiesta Bowl. The Seminoles cracked under pressure, the pressure of Tennessee's defense.

The centerpiece of the defensive gem: Heralded Florida State receiver Peter Warrick was held to just one catch for seven yards.

The Vols put the game away with $1^1/_2$ minutes left as Steve Johnson snuffed out Florida State's last chances with an interception to wrap up a 23-16 victory for the national championship.

•**RELIEVER:** FSU quarterback Marcus Outzen (14) ran for 1 TD and passed for 145 yards but it wasn't enough to lead FSU to victory.

The Road to No. 1

The Fiesta Bowl

● **SPECIAL MOMENT: Defensive back Willie Miles (3) led the end zone chanting of UT fans after the game.**

"You saw the best defense in the country tonight," UT linebacker Eric Westmoreland said.

"They're probably tearing the town up in Knoxville now. We showed we could play them straight up man-to-man. The key was to stop the run and make Marcus Outzen make big plays."

In the first half, UT cornerback Dwayne Goodrich stepped in front of an Outzen pass intended for Warrick and returned it 54 yards for a touchdown.

In the second half with the Vols leading, 20-9, Shaun Ellis stripped the ball from Outzen and Billy Ratliff recovered to set up a fourth-quarter UT field goal.

UT's victory set off a wild celebration at Sun Devil Stadium.

"I can see why nobody won up there (in Knoxville)," FSU offensive guard Jason Whitaker said. "If they can make that much noise just bringing half their stadium, that's unbelievable.

"I feel more like we lost this game than they won it. It was a case of us letting it slip through our fingers rather than getting beat. Our whole offense was sloppy all night long. We had a good enough offense to beat Tennessee. There was no reason for us to play like we did. We had entirely too many penalties and they say if you keep making the same mistakes you're just stupid. I guess that's what we are.

"It was probably the worst the offensive line has played all year long. I'm supposed to be the leader of the offensive line, so I'll take the blame for the loss."

Westmoreland was a pain in Florida State's side with three tackles for minus yardage.

"I thought Steve Johnson and Dwayne Goodrich stepped it up real big against Peter Warrick," Westmoreland said.

● **KEY PLAY: Dwayne Goodrich's 54-yard pass interception for a TD (left) was the turning point in the game.**

The Fiesta Bowl

● SALUTE: Receivers Peerless Price (37) and Steve Johnson (right) savor the feeling of finally being crowned National Champions.

The Road to No. 1

1998 Tennessee Volunteers

National Champion Vols

NO.	NAME	POS.	HT.	WT.	ELIG.	EXP	HOMETOWN (HIGH SCHOOL/JC)
1	Robert Loudermilk	PK	6-2	164	Jr.	—	Brentwood (Brentwood)
2	Fred White	DB	5-11	185	Jr.	2L	Griffin, Ga. (Griffin)
3	Willie Miles	DB	6-0	170	Fr.	—	Fort Worth, Texas (Dunbar)
4	Jeff Hall	PK	6-0	182	Sr.	3L	Winchester (Franklin Co.)
5	Burney Veazey	QB	6-2	195	Fr.	—	Southhaven, Miss. (Sou. Baptist)
6	Jeremaine Copeland	WR	6-2	200	Sr.	3L	Harriman (Harriman)
7	Deon Grant	DB	6-3	190	So.	1L	Augusta, Ga. (Josey)
8	Joey Mathews	QB	6-3	210	Fr.	—	Sevierville (Sevier Co.)
9	Steven Marsh	DB	6-1	175	Fr.	—	Wingate, N.C. (Forest Hills)
10	Benson Scott	H	6-0	193	Sr.	1L	Knoxville (Farragut)
11	Bobby Graham	WR	6-0	185	Fr.	—	Statesville, N.C. (Statesville)
12	Teddy Gaines	DB	6-0	160	Fr.	—	Kingsport (Dobyns-Bennett)
13	Tad Golden	DB	6-1	185	Fr.	—	Lithonia, Ga. (SW DeKalb)
14	Cedrick Wilson	WR	5-10	165	So.	—	Memphis (Melrose)
15	Tim Sewell	DB	5-11	178	Sr.	3L	Columbia (Central)
17	Tee Martin	QB	6-3	215	Jr.	2L	Mobile, Ala. (Williamson)
18	Gerald Griffin	DB	6-1	182	Jr.	2L	Murfreesboro (Riverdale)
19	Shawn Seabrooks	DB	5-9	185	Fr.	—	Paterson, N.J. (Eastside)
20	Travis Henry	RB	5-11	212	So.	1L	Frostproof, Fla. (Frostproof)
21	Phillip Crosby	RB	6-1	243	Jr.	1L	Bessemer City, N.C. (Coffeyville CC)
22	Corey Terry	DE	6-3	250	Sr.	2L	Warrenton, N.C. (Garden City CC)
23	Dwayne Goodrich	DB	6-0	185	Jr.	2L	Oak Lawn, Ill. (Richard)
24	Shawn Bryson	RB	6-1	220	Sr.	3L	Franklin, N.C. (Franklin)
25	Travis Stephens	RB	5-9	185	So.	1L	Clarksville (Northeast)
26	Leonard Scott	WR	5-11	165	Fr.	—	Zachary, La. (Zachary)
27	Al Wilson	LB	6-0	226	Sr.	3L	Jackson (Central-Merry)
28	Dominique Stevenson	LB	6-0	205	So.	Sq.	Gaffney, S.C. (Gaffney)
29	Mikki Allen	DB	6-0	175	Jr.	2L	Murfreesboro (Brentwood Acad.)
30	Andre Lott	DB	5-11	185	So.	Sq.	Memphis (Melrose)
33	Derrick Edmonds	DB	5-10	185	Jr.	2L	Tampa, Fla. (Hillsborough)
34	Steve Johnson	DB	5-11	175	Sr.	3L	Powder Springs, Ga. (McEachern)
35	Shawn Johnson	LB	6-2	217	Jr.	2L	Louisville, Ky. (Trinity)
36	Maurice Fitzgerald	DB	5-9	180	Fr.	Sq.	Nashville (Pearl-Cohn)
37	Peerless Price	WR	6-0	183	Sr.	3L	Dayton, Ohio (Meadowdale)
38	Roger Alexander	DE	6-3	220	Jr.	Tr.	Paterson, N.J. (Nassau CC)
39	Andre James	LB	6-2	210	Fr.	Sq.	Harmony, N.C. (North Iredell)
40	Billy Ratliff	DT	6-3	275	Jr.	2L	Magnolia, Miss. (South Pike)
41	Chris Ramseur	LB	5-10	211	So.	1L	Maiden, N.C. (Maiden)
42	Eric Westmoreland	LB	6-0	210	So.	1L	Jasper (Marion Co.)
43	David Leaverton	P	6-4	210	So.	Sq.	Midland, Texas (Midland)
44	Austin Kemp	LB	6-2	220	So.	1L	Brentwood (Brentwood Academy)
45	Will Bartholomew	RB	6-0	220	Fr.	Sq.	Nashville (Mongomery Bell Academy.)
46	Raynoch Thompson	LB	6-3	217	Jr.	1L	New Orleans, La. (St. Augustine)
47	Kurston Biggers	RB	5-7	188	Fr.	—	Nashville (Brentwood Academy)
48	Bill Hurst	P	5-11	170	Sr.	Sq.	Brentwood (Brentwood)

The Road to No. 1

NO.	NAME	POS.	HT.	WT.	ELIG.	EXP	HOMETOWN (HIGH SCHOOL/JC)
50	Keyon Whiteside	LB	6-2	230	Fr.	—	Forest City, N.C. (Chase)
51	Kevin Gregory	DS	6-4	270	Jr.	1L	Union, S.C. (Union)
52	Cosey Coleman	OG	6-5	315	So.	1L	Clarkston, Ga. (SW DeKalb)
53	Toby Champion	OG	6-4	295	So.	Sq.	Humboldt (Humboldt)
54	Diron Robinson	C	6-3	295	Sr.	3L	Oklahoma City, Okla. (Midwest City)
55	Ron Green	DT	6-1	275	Sr.	3L	Severna Park, Md. (Severna Park)
56	Bernard Jackson	LB	6-4	245	Fr.	—	Louisville, Ky. (St. Xavier)
57	Travis Colston	LB	6-3	220	Fr.	—	Marshville, N.C. (Forest Hills)
58	Darwin Walker	DT	6-3	281	Jr.	1L	Walterboro, S.C. (Walterboro)
59	Judd Granzow	LB	6-4	235	So.	JC	Granada Hills, Calif. (Moorpark CC)
60	Matt Goodin	DT	6-0	255	Sr.	Sq.	Englewood (McMinn Central)
63	Josh Campbell	DS	6-2	250	Sr.	Sq.	Knoxville (Halls)
66	Thomas Stallworth	LB	6-2	220	Fr.	Sq.	Lithonia, Ga. (Lithonia)
67	Chad Clifton	OT	6-6	315	Jr.	2L	Martin (Westview)
68	Spencer Riley	C	6-3	295	Jr.	2L	New Market (Jefferson Co.)
69	Ethan Massa	OG	6-3	285	So.	Sq.	Cookeville (Chattanooga Baylor)
71	Reggie Coleman	OT	6-5	300	Fr.	Sq.	Jonesboro, Ark. (Jonesboro)
72	Jarvis Reado	OT	6-5	300	Sr.	2L	Marrero, La. (Shaw)
73	Will Ofenheusle	OT	6-8	305	Fr.	—	Martin (Westview)
74	Bernard Gooden	OG	6-3	310	So.	Sq.	Bradenton, Fla. (Manatee)
75	Mercedes Hamilton	OG	6-3	295	Sr.	3L	Waynesboro, Ga. (Fork Union Acad.)
76	Justin Satterfield	DE	6-3	230	Fr.	Sq.	Knoxville (Halls)
77	Josh Tucker	OT	6-4	295	Jr.	2L	Asheville, N.C. (Roberson)
78	Tim Hodges	OT	6-8	295	Fr.	—	Winnie, Texas (East Chambers)
79	Reggie Ridley	DT	6-4	270	Fr.	—	Nashville (Pearl-Cohn)
80	Eric Parker	WR	6-0	163	Fr.	Sq.	Shorewood, Ill. (Joliet Township)
81	Edward Kendrick	TE	6-4	240	Fr.	—	Macon, Ga. (Mt. DeSales Academy)
82	Eric Diogu	TE	6-3	245	Jr.	2L	Garland, Tex. (Lakeview Centennial)
83	Tyrone Graham	DB	5-9	160	So.	Sq.	High Point, N.C. (Andrews)
84	Neil Johnson	TE	6-4	250	So.	Sq.	Nashville (Franklin Road Academy)
85	Donte' Stallworth	WR	6-2	180	Fr.	—	Sacramento, Calif. (Grant)
86	Kevin Taylor	WR	5-10	175	Fr.	Sq.	Memphis (Melrose)
87	David Martin	WR	6-4	210	So.	1L	Norfolk, Va. (Norview)
88	Jermaine Kent	WR	6-2	180	Fr.	—	Huntsville, Ala. (Johnson)
90	Will Overstreet	DE	6-4	250	Fr.	—	Jackson, Miss. (Jackson Prep)
91	Omari Hand	DE	6-5	215	Fr.	—	Tallahassee, Fla. (Lincoln)
92	Jeff Coleman	DT	6-4	242	Sr.	3L	Gaffney, S.C. (Gaffney)
93	Shaun Ellis	DE	6-4	260	Jr.	1L	Anderson, S.C. (Westside)
94	Ed Butler	DE	6-3	230	Fr.	Sq.	Huntsville, Ala. (Johnson)
95	Fred Weary	DT	6-4	281	Fr.	Sq.	Montgomery, Ala. (Robert E. Lee)
96	John Finlayson	TE	6-4	270	Fr.	Sq.	Selmer (McNairy Central)
97	Joe Reid	DE	6-5	220	Fr.	—	Goodlettsville (Goodpasture)
98	Antron Peebles	TE	6-3	247	Sr.	2L	Murfreesboro (Riverdale)
99	DeAngelo Lloyd	DE	6-5	235	So.	1L	Charlotte, N.C. (Independence)

1998 Statistics

TEAM*

	UT	Opp
First downs	234	203
Rushing	121	81
Passing	94	105
Penalty	19	17
Rushing attempts	517	420
Yards gained	2,825	1,634
Yards lost	289	507
Net yards rushing	2,536	1127
Net yards passing	2,250	2,509
Attempts	275	406
Completed	157	213
Had intercepted	7	16
Total offensive plays	792	826
Total net yards	4,786	3,636
Sacks by	31	23
Fumbles-lost	23-10	33-17
Penalties-yards	72-597	82-689
Interceptions-yards	16-242	7-80
Punts-yards	57-2,201	68-2,761
Punts average	38.9	40.6
Punt returns-yards	37-208	34-383
Kickoff returns-yards	34-779	50-969
Time of possession	29:30	30:30
Third-down conversions	62-158	64-188

Scoring by Quarters

	1st	2nd	3rd	4th	OT	Total	Avg.
Tennessee	82	126	106	91	3	408	34.0
Opponents	30	37	41	65	0	173	14.4

*Through 12 games

The Road to No. 1

INDIVIDUAL *

Rushing

	Att.	Yards	TDs	Long
Henry	176	970	7	36
Lewis	73	497	3	67
Stephens	107	477	4	30
T. Martin	103	287	7	55
Bryson	21	200	4	58
Crosby	16	53	2	20
Bartholomew	7	34	0	14
Price	3	25	0	12
Graham	2	-3	0	1
Veazey	9	-4	0	15

Passing

	Com.	Att.	Ints.	Yards	Long	TDs
T. Martin	153	267	6	2,164	71	19
Veazey	4	7	1	86	29	1
Henry	0	1	0	0	0	0

Receiving

	No.	Yards	TDs	Long
Price	61	920	10	71
C. Wilson	33	558	6	55
Copeland	29	438	1	35
Bryson	19	167	1	63
Finlayson	4	47	1	21
Henry	4	31	0	20
D. Martin	3	59	0	29
Stephens	2	3	0	5
Lewis	1	16	1	16
Taylor	1	11	0	11

Punts

	No.	Yards	Avg.	Long
Leaverton	56	2,178	38.9	61
Team	1	23	23	23

Field Goals

	Att.	Made	Long
Hall	24	19	47

All Returns

	Punts	KOs	Ints.
Price	1-(-3)	14-389	0-0
Stephens	0-0	8-169	0-0
Edmonds	0-0	5-98	2-0
C. Wilson	0-0	4-84	0-0
Goodrich	0-0	1-26	3-14
Miles	0-0	1-13	0-0
Copeland	16-68	1-0	0-0
Grant	0-0	2-11	5-79
Ellis	0-0	0-0	1-90
White	0-0	0-0	1-33
St. Johnson	0-0	0-0	1-22
A. Wilson	0-0	0-0	1-9
Griffin	0-0	0-0	1-0
Westmoreland	0-0	0-0	1-(-5)

Tackling Leaders

	Total	Solo	Asst.
Thompson	89	62	27
Westmoreland	79	60	19
Wilson	77	54	23
Grant	62	38	24
Terry	58	40	18
White	57	37	20
Walker	46	33	13
Edmonds	45	27	18
St. Johnson	43	30	13
Ramseur	42	29	13
Goodrich	41	26	15
Ellis	40	26	14
Coleman	36	20	18
Granzow	33	21	12
Ratliff	29	19	10
Lloyd	24	17	7

PHOTO CREDITS

AllSport Photography USA — *Front Cover, Back Cover, 6, 7-left, 7-center, 11, 22-23, 30-31, 38-39, 40-41, 43, 62, 64-65, 66-67, 68-69, 72-73, 80-81, 83, 84-85, 88, 93, 112-113, 116-117, 124-125, 127, 140-141, 142, 144, 146-147, 148-149, 150, 151, 153, 154, 155, 160.*

AP/Wide World — *7-right, 14-15, 17, 18, 19, 29, 32-33, 36-37, 44-45, 50, 51, 52-53, 54, 58, 63, 71, 74, 75, 76, 78-79, 90, 98, 115, 118-119, 120-121, 123, 130, 131, 132, 133, 134-both, 136-both, 137-both, 152.*

The Knoxville News-Sentinel — *4-5-both, 5-both, 8, 12-13, 20-21, 24-25, 26-27, 35, 56-57, 61, 86, 87-both, 89, 94-95, 97, 101, 102, 104, 108-109, 110-111, 111, 143.*